FAMILY CIRCLE

Quick Cross Stitch

45 BEAUTIFUL PROJECTS

MURDOCH BOOKS®
Sydney • London • Vancouver • New York

Contents

Contents

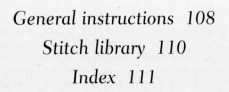

Buttons and bangles

Cross-stitched bangles are a clever way to achieve casual style.

Simple and smart: these blue and white buttons are very easy to make.

Embroidered buttons can be made in an evening and will add a new accent to a jacket or blouse. Choose from simple blue and white buttons and matching bangles, or embroider bright flag designs.

BLUE AND WHITE BUTTONS

Size About 2.5 cm in diameter

MATERIALS

For each button

10 cm square piece of blue evenweave fabric with ten fabric threads per 1 cm

DMC stranded embroidery cottons in variegated light blue (67)

Tapestry needle size 24

2.5 cm diameter self-cover button

EMBROIDERY

Following the graph, embroider the selected motif in the centre of the fabric. Work in cross stitch using two strands of the cotton. Work the crosses for motif 1 over two fabric threads, and those for motif 2 over three fabric threads.

TO ASSEMBLE

Cover the buttons with the embroidered piece, following the instructions on the packaging.

BLUE AND WHITE BANGLES

Size Width of blue motif on white bangle 3 cm, of white motif on blue bangle 4 cm

MATERIALS

12 x 30 cm bias strip of white and a 15 x 30 cm bias strip of blue evenweave cotton fabric, both with ten fabric threads per 1 cm

DMC stranded embroidery cotton in blue (796) and white

Tapestry needle size 24

3 cm and 4 cm wide bangles, with a circumference of 26 cm

EMBROIDERY

Embroider the motifs in cross stitch on the fabric, following the relevant graph (turn graph 45°). Work each cross stitch over two fabric threads using two strands of embroidery cotton. Start your embroidery 2 cm from the fabric edges for each motif. If needed, repeat a small section of graph to obtain the required length.

TO ASSEMBLE

Sew the short ends of the strip together to form a continuous piece. Fold the piece in half across its width, with wrong sides facing, and place the bangle inside. Sew the long sides together, with the raw edges turned inwards: if necessary, trim the seam before sewing.

BUTTONS WITH FLAGS

Size About 2.5 cm in diameter

MATERIALS

For each button

8 cm square piece of linen with ten fabric threads per 1 cm

Small quantities DMC stranded embroidery cottons in the colours of the required button

Tapestry needle size 24

2.5 cm diameter self-cover button

GRAPHS FOR BLUE AND WHITE BUTTONS

⊠ variegated light blue 67

MOTIF 1

MOTIF 2

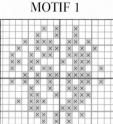

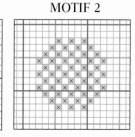

MOTIFS FOR BUTTONS WITH FLAGS

DMC COLOUR KEY

symbol	colour	no.
·	white	
■	black	310
∩	yellow	307
✕	red	666
●	dark blue	796
∧	medium blue	798

GRAPH FOR WHITE BANGLE ● blue 796

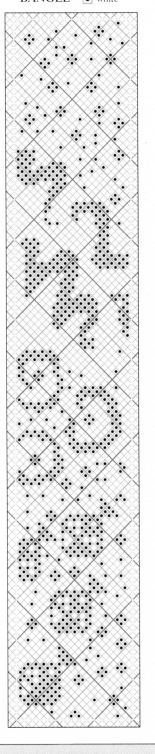

GRAPH FOR BLUE BANGLE ● white

EMBROIDERY

Following the graph, embroider the motif in cross stitch in the centre of the linen. Work each cross stitch over two fabric threads, using three strands of embroidery cotton.

TO ASSEMBLE

Cover the button with the completed embroidery, following the instructions on the packaging.

The Netherlands, Spain, the United Kingdom, Belgium and Sweden: bring Europe together with these colourful buttons.

In the frame

Colourful butterflies are always a delight to look at. Embroider the whole collection, or choose one to decorate a book cover or other small article.

PICTURE WITH NINE BUTTERFLIES

Size Picture 21 cm square; embroidered area 12.5 x 14 cm

MATERIALS

30 cm square piece of white linen with eleven fabric threads per 1 cm

DMC stranded embroidery cottons in the colours indicated on the colour key

Tapestry needle size 24

Hobby paints in pink, blue and white

Wooden frame

EMBROIDERY

Following the graph, embroider the butterflies in cross stitch. Work each cross over two fabric threads, using two strands of embroidery cotton. Start the embroidery with the outer border in the right-hand lower corner, 8 cm inside the edges. Work the border in back stitch, using two strands of dark blue (826). When all cross stitching is complete, work the outlines in back stitch, using two strands of cotton.

TO ASSEMBLE

Paint the frame pink, and leave to dry. Add white and blue painted spots. Frame the completed embroidery.

Above: Nine butterflies in a frame: all are simple to stitch and the overall effect is delightful.
Below: Choose any of the butterflies for this lovely book cover, but the blue one is certainly attractive.

6

GRAPH FOR NINE BUTTERFLIES

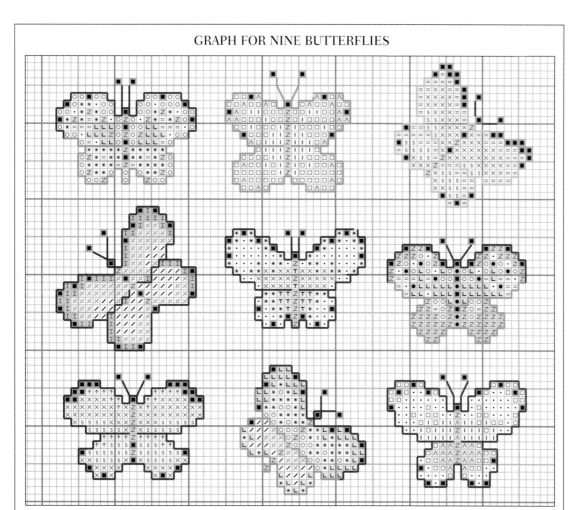

GRAPH FOR BORDER OF BOOK COVER

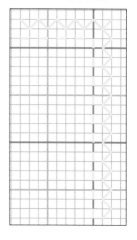

DMC COLOUR KEY

s	light yellow	3078
✗	yellow	726
═	bright yellow	444
↑	dark yellow	743
L	orange	741
✳	ecru	677
◯	light brown	676
Z	brown	3045
T	medium brown	729
●	dark brown	611
▢	light pink	818
!	pink	776
⋀	dark pink	899
⁄	light blue	828
⬕	blue	519
I	dark blue	826
■	grey	413
•	white	

OUTLINES

▢	orange	741
▢	dark brown	611
▢	grey	413
▢	pink	3326

BOOK COVER

MATERIALS

White linen with eleven threads per 1 cm, as high as the book plus 2 cm, and as wide as the width of the front, back and spine of the book combined, plus 10 cm extra

Same-sized piece of white cotton for the lining

DMC stranded embroidery cottons in grey (413), light blue (828), blue (519), dark blue (826), brown (3045) and pink (3326)

Tapestry needle size 24

Book or diary

EMBROIDERY

Following the graph, embroider the outer border along the outer edge of the linen, using pink embroidery cotton (3326): position border 1.5 cm from top and bottom edges, and 5.5 cm from the side edges. Work zig-zag line with two strands, and running stitches with four.

Following the graph for the picture, embroider the blue butterfly in cross stitch in the lower right-hand corner. Work each cross over two fabric threads, using two strands of embroidery cotton. When all cross stitching is complete, work the outlines in back stitch, using two strands of grey (413).

TO FINISH

Sew the embroidered and lining pieces together with right sides facing, leaving an opening on one short side. Cut away seam corners diagonally and turn the cover right side out. Slip stitch the opening closed. Fold short sides 4 cm inwards, and sew in place along top and bottom edges. Insert the book or diary.

Country style

Colourful flowers worked in cross stitch on linen are perfect to decorate the kitchen. Pink, blue and red flowers are set off by borders of red stitches.

Bring the garden indoors with this country-style cloth—the scattered flowers are really attractive and you needn't stitch a lot of them to achieve the effect.

TABLECLOTH

Size 80 cm square

MATERIALS

90 cm square piece of white evenweave linen with eleven threads per 1 cm

DMC stranded embroidery cottons in the colours indicated on the colour key, plus red (326)

Tapestry needle size 24

EMBROIDERY

Following the graph, embroider the motifs in cross stitch. Work each cross over two fabric threads, using two strands of embroidery cotton. Arrange the flowers over the cloth as you like. To determine their position, use small pieces of paper. Ensure you place the motifs at least 9 cm inside the outer edges of the fabric. When all cross stitching is complete, work the lines in the violas with straight stitches in black. Work

the outlines in back stitch, using one strand of cotton.

TO FINISH

Cut the cloth to measure 88 cm square. Baste a 2 cm wide double hem around the cloth, and make mitred corners. Withdraw two fabric threads above the hem, stopping at the corners where these threads intersect. Darn short ends of the threads back into the fabric. Secure the hem with open hemstitch over three fabric threads, using two strands of red (326).

MOTIFS FOR TABLECLOTH

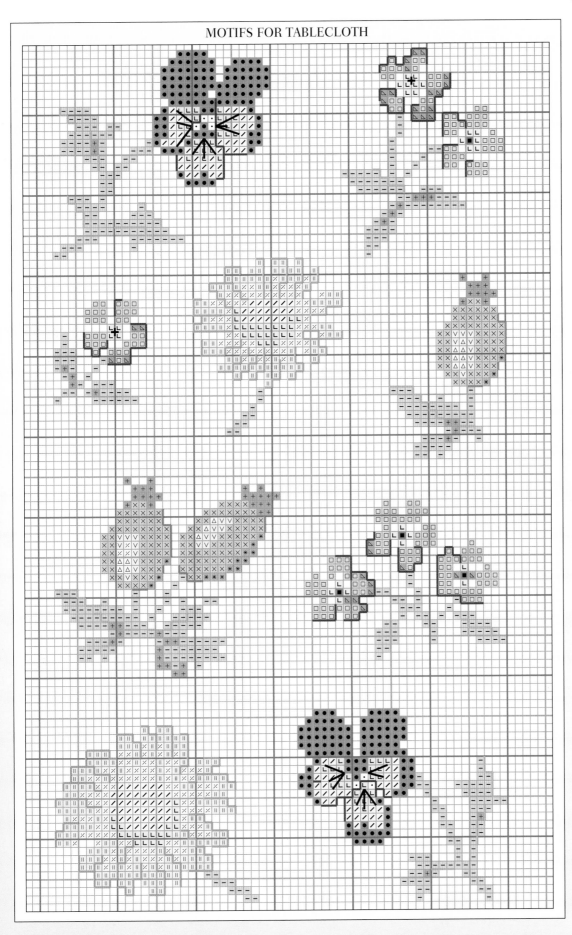

DMC COLOUR KEY

∕	light yelllow	727
L	yellow	743
⊠	light pink	818
‖	pink	3326
−	light green	3348
+	green	988
□	light blue	809
◹	blue	798
●	dark blue	791
■	black	310
△	very light pink	948
∨	light red	353
⊠	red	351
＊	dark red	349
⊡	white	

OUTLINES

▢	light green	3348
▢	dark blue	791
▢	black	310
▢	dark red	349
▢	dark pink	335

9

NAPKIN RING

Size About 5 cm wide

MATERIALS

For one ring

12.5.x 15.5 cm piece of white evenweave linen with eleven threads per 1 cm

DMC stranded embroidery cottons in the colours of the three blue flowers motif, plus red (326)

Tapestry needle size 24

One small button

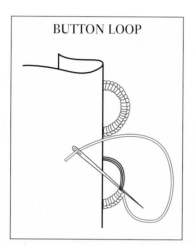

BUTTON LOOP

EMBROIDERY

Cut the linen into two pieces 6.25 x 15.5 cm. Following the graph, embroider the motif of the three blue flowers in the centre of one piece of linen. Work in cross stitch over two fabric threads, using two strands of embroidery cotton. When all cross stitching is complete, work the outlines in back stitch, using one strand of cotton. Using red (326), work a row of cross stitches along the top and bottom of the flower motif, leaving a space of two fabric threads between each cross: position the rows four fabric threads outside the outermost crosses of the motif.

TO FINISH

Using 5 mm wide seams, sew the embroidered piece and plain piece together with right sides facing, along one short and two long sides. Turn right side out and sew other end closed. To close napkin ring, make a button loop on one end, and sew a button to correspond on other end.

SHELF BORDERS

Size About 6 cm wide

MATERIALS

Piece of 6 cm wide white evenweave linen band with eleven threads per 1 cm, as long as required plus 2 cm extra for hems

DMC stranded embroidery cottons in the colours of the selected motifs, as indicated on the colour key, plus red (326) for the outer borders

Tapestry needle size 24

METHOD

Work a row of cross stitches along the top and bottom edges of the band: position these two fabric threads inside the edges, and leave a space of two fabric threads between each cross. Work the crosses over two fabric threads, using two strands of the red (326) embroidery cotton. Following the various graphs, embroider the flower motifs in the centre of the band: work

Napkin rings with flowers and cross-stitched borders look lovely with the embroidered tablecloth but can also be used with a plain blue or green one.

either the different blue flowers, or a border of alternating blue, red, blue and pink flowers. Leave 1.25 cm between each motif, and repeat the motifs until the required length is reached. When all the cross stitching is complete, work the outlines in back stitch, using one strand of cotton.

Finish the ends of the borders with a narrow hem.

The final touch in a country-style kitchen: shelf borders with rows of pretty flowers.

This pretty
coathanger—
just waiting for that
special party dress—
can be made in any size
you like.

A little romance

MATERIALS

Coathanger

Small piece of white chintz

Thin batting

Small quantities of DMC stranded embroidery cottons in pink (776), yellow (744), sea green (964) and blue (3325)

Crewel needle size 8

Small piece of 14-count waste canvas (fourteen stitches to 2.5 cm)

40 cm of 4 cm wide pink ribbon

White broderie anglaise

Basting thread

Pattern paper

PATTERN

Place the coathanger on the paper, and draw around the shape of the top and edges; extend the lines slightly and draw a straight line across the bottom. Cut out the paper pattern. Place it on the white chintz (along the grain) and cut out, adding a 1.5 cm seam allowance. Place the waste canvas over the remaining chintz (along the grain) and baste in place. Position the paper pattern on this (two-layered) piece, and outline the pattern shape with running stitches. Cut out 5 cm from the marked lines.

EMBROIDERY

Following the graph, embroider the desired name and the flowers within the marked outlines of the two-layered piece in cross stitch. Work each cross through both layers, over two canvas threads, using two strands of embroidery cotton. Keep the needle perpendicular to the canvas while working, and stitch only through the canvas holes, not the canvas threads. Work the name in pink, and surround it with flower motifs as desired. Work the petals of each flower in one colour only (sea-green, blue or pink), and the centres in yellow. When stitching is completed, dampen the canvas, and remove the basting and the canvas threads one by one with tweezers.

TO ASSEMBLE

Place the two chintz pieces with right sides together, and sew the top and side edges with 1 cm wide seam, leaving a 1.5 cm wide opening in the centre at the top edge (the cover will now be 5 mm wider than the hanger, to allow for the thickness of hanger). Clip all seam curves and turn the cover right side out.

Calculate twice the circumference of the lower edge of the cover, and cut the lace to that length. Sew the ends together, forming a continuous piece, and gather the top edge. Sew the lace to the lower edge of the cover and topstitch closely along the edge of the cover. Cover the coathanger with batting, securing it with a few stitches. Place the cover over the coathanger. Knot the ribbon around the top of the hook and tie into a bow.

This coathanger is covered in chintz, trimmed with broderie anglaise and decorated with cross-stitch embroidery. It's a perfect gift for little girls, but it's just as suitable for romantics of any age.

ALPHABET FOR COATHANGER

DMC COLOUR KEY

☒ pink   776

◉ yellow   744

Mother goose

Wearing bonnets and headscarfs, these plump white geese embroidered on a tablecloth and oven glove make a cheerful addition to the kitchen.

Use a round or square tablecloth for this project and embroider four or eight geese as you please.

TABLECLOTH

Size About 85 cm square

MATERIALS

90 cm square piece of white closely woven linen fabric

DMC stranded embroidery cottons in the colours indicated on the colour key, on page 16

Crewel needle size 8

Eight 15 cm square pieces of 10-count waste canvas (ten stitches to 2.5 cm)

EMBROIDERY

Making running stitches, mark a 50 cm diameter circle in the centre of the cloth. Divide the circle into eight equal sections, by working one horizontal, one vertical and two diagonal lines.

Following the graph, embroider eight geese in cross stitch. To do this, baste a 15 cm square piece of waste canvas over the area: the legs of the geese should be positioned against the circle, and the geese centred on the radiating lines. Work four

geese without dresses on the horizontal and vertical marked lines. Work the scarf alternately in blue and green. Between these, on the diagonal lines, work the four geese in dresses.

Work each cross stitch, through both layers, over two canvas threads, using three strands of embroidery cotton. Keep the needle perpendicular to the canvas while working, and stitch only through the holes of the canvas, not the canvas threads. When all cross

wide double hem around the cloth, making mitred corners. Secure the hem against the back of the row of stem stitches.

OVEN GLOVE

Size About 20 x 28 cm

MATERIALS

30 x 50 cm piece of blue-checked white Aida fabric with 4.5 squares per 1 cm

30 x 50 cm piece each of white cotton and batting

DMC stranded embroidery cottons in the colours of the required motif (page 16)

Tapestry needle size 24

70 cm of 2 cm wide blue bias binding

7 x 35 cm piece of blue chintz (for the bow)

70 cm of 5.5 cm wide white broderie anglaise

CUTTING OUT

Enlarge the pattern graph on page 17 and cut out the pattern piece. On Aida fabric outline the pattern twice, once reversed. Note the position of the squares, and if necessary, refer to the photograph. Cut out the reversed piece with 1 cm seam

In bonnet and dress, or in a bright headscarf, these geese will provide a colourful topic of conversation at the table.

stitching is complete, work the outlines in back stitch, using two strands of cotton.

When the embroidery is completed, dampen the canvas, and remove the basting and the waste canvas threads one by one with tweezers.

TO FINISH

Mark an 81 cm frame around the linen, by withdrawing one fabric thread. Work a row of stem stitch over the obtained lines, using two strands of blue cotton (798). Baste a 1.5 cm

allowance, but without seam on the lower edge.

Also cut out the pattern once from double cotton fabric and once from double batting, adding 5 mm seams except on the lower edge.

EMBROIDERY

Following the graph, embroider the motif on the marked but uncut piece of Aida fabric, referring to the photo for its position. Work each cross over one fabric square, using two strands of

embroidery cotton, also working over the blue lines of the checks. When all cross stitching is complete, work the outlines in back stitch, using one strand of cotton, but work the beak with two strands. Cut out the mitten

MOTHER GOOSE MOTIFS

DMC COLOUR KEY		
⊡	white	
■	black	310
◩	red	605
◬	green	704
◪	dark blue	796
●	blue	798
∅	light blue	809
⊠	orange	947
▨	pink	962
∩	light pink	963
☑	dark yellow	972

OUTLINES		
☐	red	605
☐	dark blue	796
☐	blue	798
☐	yellow	743
☐	golden yellow	972

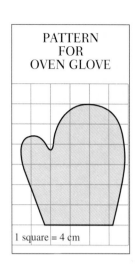

*The oven glove is
finished with romantic
lace and a bow.*

shape, allowing 1 cm seam except on the lower edge.

THE GLOVE

For the glove lining, place the cotton and batting pieces together with the cotton ones on the outside, and using a 1 cm wide seam, sew all four pieces together. For the outside of the glove, sew the two Aida pieces together with right sides facing, using 1 cm wide seam. Trim the seams and clip the seam curves. Turn right side out, and place the glove lining inside. Finish the lower edges of the glove with bias binding all around.

From bias binding cut a 10 cm long loop. Fold the piece double across its width and sew the long sides together.

THE FRILL

Sew short ends of the broderie lace together to form a continuous piece, and secure the short seam sections with a turning against the wrong side. Gather the frill to measure 28 cm.

Press the seam fold open on one side of the remaining bias binding. Sew it into a ring with 1.5 cm seam. With right sides facing, sew the lace and bias binding together (the lace should extend 5 mm outside the bias binding), and sew exactly over the pressed fold. Fold the bias binding over the seam, and sew in place. Baste it to the right side of the outer glove 1 cm from the lower edge. Sew frill onto outer glove, closely along the edge of the bias binding, at the same time

joining folded bias binding loop on the inside to form a hanger.

TO FINISH

For the bow, cut from chintz one 7 x 30 cm strip and one 4.5 x 6 cm strip. Fold each piece in half with right sides facing. Sew the long sides together, leaving a small opening in the centre. Press the seam open and press it towards centre back. Close the short ends of the large piece diagonally, and close the ends of the small piece with straight seams. Fold the strips right side out, and sew the opening of each closed. Form the large strip into a bow, place the small strip around the centre and sew the short ends together at the back.

Sew bow on bias binding.

Add a touch of marine style with these simple anchor motifs. They can be easily added to ready-bought clothes or worked in rows on hardanger or Aida band. They're suitable, too, for any bathroom or beach article.

Anchors aweigh

EMBROIDERY

Baste the waste canvas over the area to be embroidered. Following the graph, embroider the motif in cross stitch. Work each cross through both layers over two canvas threads, using two strands of embroidery cotton. Keep the needle perpendicular to the canvas while working, and stitch only through the canvas holes, not the canvas threads. When completed, dampen the canvas, and remove the basting and canvas threads one by one with tweezers.

SOCKS

MATERIALS

Cotton socks

DMC stranded embroidery cottons in red (666), light blue (809) and blue (796)

EMBROIDERY

Following the graph, embroider the anchor motif in cross stitch on the outer leg side of the sock. Work each cross over one knitted stitch of the sock, using two strands of embroidery cotton. When completed, work two rows of stem stitches respectively 0.5 and 1.5 cm from the top edge of the socks: work each stem stitch over two knitted stitches, using two strands of cotton in light blue (809).

Nautical flair is easy to achieve with this cross-stitched anchor motif: it's the final touch for sailor dress or hat.

HAT AND DRESS

Size Motif about 4.5 x 5 cm

MATERIALS

Knit hat or cotton dress

DMC stranded embroidery cottons in red (666) and blue (796)

Crewel needle size 8

8 cm square piece of 14-count waste canvas (fourteen stitches to 2.5 cm)

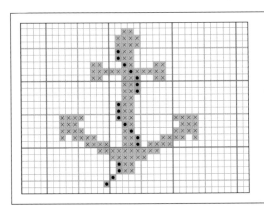

ANCHOR
MOTIF

DMC COLOUR
KEY

☒	red	666
⊙	blue	796

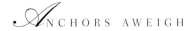

Complete your marine-style outfit by adding an anchor to purchased socks.

SHEET BORDER WITH BOATS

Size Band 6 cm wide

MATERIALS

6 cm wide white hardanger band with about ten double fabric threads per 1 cm

DMC stranded embroidery cottons in the colours indicated on the colour key

Tapestry needle size 24

EMBROIDERY

Following the graph, embroider the border in cross stitch on the hardanger band. Work each cross over two double fabric threads, using three strands of embroidery cotton. Position the boats fourteen double fabric threads from the bottom edge, and repeat the design until the required length is reached.

TO FINISH

Sew the completed band onto the sheet, about 7 cm from the top edge, with the short edges turned under.

Pairs of boats skud across hardanger band, ready to be added to sheet or towel.

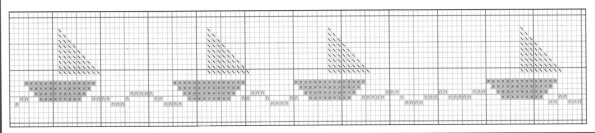

BOAT MOTIF

DMC COLOUR KEY

⋒	light green	993
⊼	light blue	794
☒	blue	798

Cactus flowers

This gorgeous sewing set of needlecase, scissors case and pincushion is decorated in contemporary style with prickly cactus plants in full flower.

NEEDLECASE

Size 7.5 x 8.5 cm; motif 4.5 x 6 cm

MATERIALS

20 x 15 cm piece of pale green 14-count Aida fabric

20 x 15 cm piece of lining fabric

12 x 6.5 piece of white felt

DMC stranded embroidery cottons in the colours indicated on the colour key, plus medium green (701)

Tapestry needle size 24

30 cm of 6 mm wide green ribbon

EMBROIDERY

With running stitches mark a 15 x 8.5 cm rectangle on the Aida fabric. Following the graph for the border, embroider the outer frame within the outline, using medium green (701). Work in cross stitch over one fabric square, using two strands of cotton. Use running stitches to mark off the right-hand 7.5 cm

CACTUS MOTIFS

DMC COLOUR KEY

⋒ light ochre	402	⟋ pink	604	● dark green	910	OUTLINES		
⁒ yellow	444	✕ light green	702	↑ dark ochre	922	☐ dark green	910	

This needlecase is pretty and practical, too.

of the fabric (this will be the front of the needlecase) and, following the main graph, work the chosen cactus motif in the centre of this rectangle in cross stitch. Work the spines of the cactus in straight stitch, using two strands of medium green (701). When completed, cut the embroidered piece 1 cm from the marked outline.

TO ASSEMBLE

Cut the lining the same size as the embroidered piece, and cut the ribbon into two equal pieces. Place the felt on the right side of the lining piece, with centres matched. Sew in place across the centre with a vertical row of stitching. Sew the lining and embroidered piece together with right sides

facing, leaving an opening for turning on one side, at the same time joining a piece of ribbon in the centre of each short side, with the raw edges aligned. Cut away seam corners. Turn the piece right side out, and sew the opening closed. Fold the needlecase double and close it with the pieces of ribbon tied into a bow.

GRAPH FOR BORDER

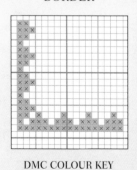

DMC COLOUR KEY
✕ medium green 701

21

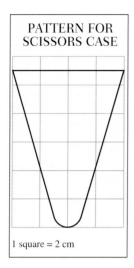

**PATTERN FOR
SCISSORS CASE**

1 square = 2 cm

*What could be more
delightful than this
prickly pincushion.*

SCISSORS CASE

Size 11 x 7.5 cm; motif
5.5 x 4 cm

MATERIALS

12 x 30 cm piece of pale green
14-count Aìda fabric

12 x 30 cm piece of matching
lining fabric

DMC stranded embroidery
cottons in the colours indicated
on the colour key, plus medium
green (701)

Tapestry needle size 24

30 cm of 6 mm wide green
ribbon

EMBROIDERY

Trace the pattern onto tracing
paper and cut out the paper pattern. Using running stitches
outline the shape of the pattern
once on Aida fabric. Cut out with
generous seam allowance. Also,
cut the pattern once from Aida
fabric adding 1 cm wide seam
allowance on the sides, and
1.5 cm on the straight top edge.

Following the graphs, embroider the border and the cactus
motif in cross stitch. Work each
cross over one fabric square,
using two strands of embroidery
cotton. Position the border within the straight top edge of the
marked shape, and the cactus

motif in the centre of the
shape. Work the border in
medium green (701). Work
the spines of the cactus in
straight stitch, using two
strands of medium green. When
completed, cut the embroidered
piece 1 cm from the marked line
at the sides, and 1.5 cm from the
straight line at the top.

TO ASSEMBLE

Cut the pattern twice from lining
fabric, adding 1 cm seam
allowance all around. Separately
sew together two lining and two
Aida pieces with right sides facing, making 1 cm wide seams.
Trim the seams and cut away the
seam point. Turn the Aida piece
right side out. Place the lining
inside the Aida piece, with wrong
sides together. Fold the top edge
of the Aida piece inwards and,
making a narrow turning, sew in
place against the lining. Cut the
ribbon in two equal pieces. Sew
the pieces opposite each other
inside the top edge of the scissors
case, with the raw edge turned
under. Insert scissors, and close
the case by tying the pieces of
ribbon into a bow.

PINCUSHION

Size 9 cm diameter; motif
5.5 x 4 cm

MATERIALS

14 cm square piece of pale
green 14-count Aida fabric

12 cm square piece of matching fabric for the back

35 cm of green cord

DMC stranded embroidery
cottons in the colours indicated
on the colour key, plus
medium green (701)

Tapestry needle size 24

Polyester fibre fill

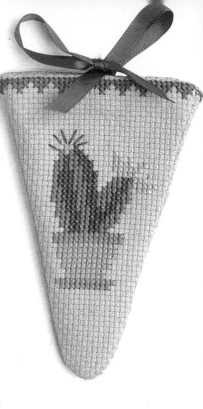

*Keep your scissors safely encased
in this holder.*

EMBROIDERY

With running stitches, mark a
9 cm diameter circle in the centre of the Aida fabric. Following
the graph, embroider the motif
in the centre of the marked circle. Work in cross stitch over
one fabric square, using two
strands of embroidery cotton.
Work the spines of the cactus in
straight stitch, using two
strands of medium green (701).
When the embroidery has been
completed, cut the piece 1 cm
outside the marked line.

TO ASSEMBLE

Cut the backing the same shape
as the embroidered piece. Sew
the two pieces together with
right sides facing, leaving a
small opening for turning and
filling. Clip the seam curves
and turn right side out. Insert
filling. Sew the cord over the
seam on the outside, with the
cord ends pushed inside the
opening, and close the opening
at the same time.

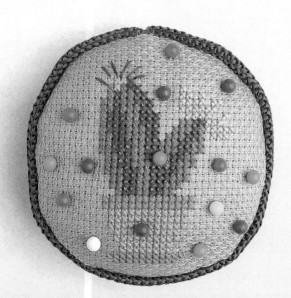

Berry red

Bright red cranberries make a delicious cover for a jar of jam.

DMC COLOUR KEY

V	dark green	701
/	light green	704
%	green	702
●	dark red	816
⊥	light red	349
X	red	321
Z	brown	975
O	orange-red	606

Size About 18 cm diameter

MATERIALS

20 x 20 cm piece of pink linen with about eleven threads per 1 cm, or pink 14-count Aida fabric

About 50 cm of 90 cm wide dotted cotton fabric

DMC stranded embroidery cottons in the colours indicated on the colour key

Tapestry needle size 24

EMBROIDERY

Following the graph, embroider the motif in the centre of the pink fabric. Work in cross stitch over two fabric threads (or one Aida square), using two strands of embroidery cotton.

TO ASSEMBLE

From dotted fabric cut one band 50 x 2 cm (for tie), one band 55 x 2 cm (cut on the bias) and an 18 cm diameter circle. Cut the embroidered piece into an 18 cm diameter circle, with motif in centre. Sew it and dotted circle together with wrong sides facing. Sew bias binding around pink piece, with right sides facing. Fold bias binding halfway over to the back, and sew in place with a narrow turning.

To make the ties, turn the raw long edges 5 mm under, fold the band double, and sew the long edges together, then make a knot in each short end.

MOTIF FOR CRANBERRIES

Holidays can be the perfect time for some cross stitching. Fill a quiet hour or two embroidering shells or mussels for a most original card, or add an embroidered band to towel or toilet bag. They will make lovely bon voyage gifts, too!

Remember friends at home with these lovely cross-stitched cards.

Bon voyage

NOTE CARDS

Size Card 12 x 16 cm; mussel motif about 4 x 4.5 cm, shell motif about 4.5 x 5 cm

MATERIALS

For one card

12 x 16 cm piece of thin blue or beige cardboard or strong paper

12 x 16 cm piece of thin white paper

10 cm square piece of white evenweave linen with ten fabric threads per 1 cm

DMC stranded embroidery cottons in the colours indicated on the colour key

Tapestry needle size 24

Craft glue

Craft knife

EMBROIDERY

Following the graph, embroider the desired motif in the centre of the fabric in cross stitch. Work each cross over two fabric threads, using two strands of

A border of mussels turns a plain towel into a stylish beach accessory.

MUSSEL MOTIF

DMC COLOUR KEY

⊡	white	
⊞	dark lavender	209
⊟	light lavender	211
◥	grey	415
⬤	dark blue	939

SHELL MOTIF

DMC COLOUR KEY

⊟	white	
·	light pink	225
⊞	brown	437
Ⅰ	beige	738
⊠	pink	754
⊙	grey	762

OUTLINES

☐	dark pink	316

embroidery cotton. When completed, work the outlines for the shell in back stitch, using one strand of dark pink (316).

To finish

Cut away a neat 4.5 x 5.5 cm window in the blue card, and a 5.5 x 6 cm window in the beige card. Position each window in the centre, 3.5 cm from the top edge (one short side). Glue embroidery behind the window, and glue white paper to the back of the card. Write your message on the lower part of the card.

TOWEL BORDER

Size Mussel motif about 3.5 cm square

MATERIALS

50 cm wide blue-grey bath towel

55 cm of 6 cm wide white hardanger band with ten double fabric threads per 1 cm

DMC stranded embroidery cottons in the colours indicated on the colour key

Tapestry needle size 24

EMBROIDERY

Following the graph, embroider mussel motifs in centre of hardanger band in cross stitch. Work each cross over two double fabric threads, using two strands of embroidery cotton. Start your embroidery about 8 cm from one end of band. Repeat motif four times, allowing 4 cm space between each motif.

To finish

Turn raw ends under, and sew embroidered band onto towel, about 6 cm from top edge.

TOILET BAG

Size 19 x 32 cm

MATERIALS

35 cm white hardanger band with ten double fabric threads per 1 cm

DMC stranded embroidery cottons in the colours indicated on the colour key

Tapestry needle size 24

FOR TOILET BAG

50 cm of 90 cm wide striped cotton

32 x 47 cm piece of plain cotton (lining)

Iron-on interfacing

Small strip of leather for the zipper tab 35 cm long zipper

2.5 m long piece of wide bias binding

EMBROIDERY

Following the graph, embroider the motif in the centre of the hardanger band in cross stitch. Start your embroidery 4 cm from the right-hand side, and work each cross over two double fabric threads, using two strands of embroidery cotton. When all cross stitching is complete, work the outlines in back stitch, using two strands of dark brown (433). Embroider four more motifs, allowing fourteen double fabric threads space between each motif. When completed, cut the band to measure 32 cm (or the

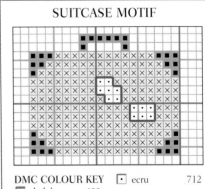

This band of embroidered suitcases can be added to any cotton toilet bag, whether bought or handmade.

width of your bag), with the motifs in the centre.

CUTTING OUT

From the striped cotton cut one 32 x 45 cm piece for the outer bag, one 32 cm square piece for the inside pocket, and four 9 x 17 cm strips for the gussets.

TO ASSEMBLE

Reinforce the outer bag piece with the iron-on interfacing. Place the gussets together two by two with wrong sides facing, and finish one short side of both pieces with bias binding. Finish two opposite sides of the pocket with bias binding. Place the pocket on the lining piece: position it with raw edges even, and the finished sides of the pocket 7.5 cm from the top and bottom edges (short sides) of the lining piece.

Topstitch parallel to the finished sides of the pocket, using two rows of stitching, 7 cm apart, and positioning the stitching 11.5 cm from the finished sides. If preferred, also topstitch a few vertical rows, forming squares.

Pin the striped outer bag and lining bag together with wrong sides facing. Fold the piece double with the striped piece on the outside. Pin the gussets between the sides, and finish the seams with bias binding.

Place the zipper at the top of the bag: position it against the lining with the zipper teeth pointing towards the bottom of the bag, and allow the zipper to extend at one end. Sew the zipper in place. Finish the top edge and the extending zipper piece with bias binding. Knot a piece of leather around the zipper tab.

SUITCASE MOTIF

DMC COLOUR KEY			⊡ ecru	712
■ dark brown	433		OUTLINES	
⊠ light brown	437		☐ dark brown	433

Surprise family and friends with an exciting Easter gift. Make a placemat and egg warmer with fluffy chickens, or a picture with chick, eggs or bunny. The motifs are perfect for special Easter cards, too.

Easter surprises

Little cross-stitched pictures make perfect Easter gifts.

PATTERN FOR EGG WARMER

1 square = 2 cm

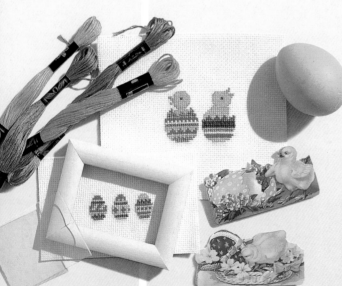

EASTER PICTURES

MATERIALS

For one picture

About 10 cm square piece of white 18-count Aida fabric

DMC stranded embroidery cottons in colours indicated on colour key

Tapestry needle size 26

Matching frame with inside measurements about 1 cm larger than the motif

EMBROIDERY

Following the graph, embroider the selected motif in the centre of the fabric. Work in cross stitch over one fabric square, using two strands of embroidery cotton. When all cross stitching is complete, work the outlines in back stitch, using one strand of cotton. Work the whiskers of the rabbit in straight stitch, using one strand of black.

EGG WARMER

Size 8 x 8.5 cm

MATERIALS

14 x 22 cm piece of white 14-count Aida fabric

14 x 22 cm piece of thick flannel

DMC stranded embroidery cottons in the colours indicated on the colour key for the placemat

Tapestry needle size 24

METHOD

Cut the Aida fabric into two equal pieces, measuring 14 x 11 cm. Enlarge the pattern for the egg warmer and cut out a paper pattern. Outline the pattern on the Aida pieces, 3 cm from the lower edge.

EMBROIDERY

Following the graph for the placemat, embroider one chicken and border in the centre of each piece, 1.5 cm from the lower marked line. When all cross stitching is complete, work the outlines in back stitch using two strands of cotton.

TO FINISH

Cut the Aida pieces 5 mm outside the marked line, but at the lower edge cut 3 cm outside the marked line. Cut the pattern twice from flannel, adding 5 mm seam all around, but omit seam on the lower edge. Sew the two Aida pieces together and the two flannel pieces together, leaving the lower edge of each pair open. Turn Aida cover right side out. Trim the seams of the flannel piece, and slide it inside

Breakfast, lunch or tea— this placemat and egg warmer will get lots of use all year round.

the cover. Fold the cover 3 cm inwards, and sew in place with a 1 cm wide turning.

PLACEMAT

Size 34 x 48 cm

MATERIALS

36 x 50 cm piece of white 11-count Aida fabric

36 x 50 cm piece of white cotton

DMC stranded embroidery cottons in the colours indicated on the colour key

Tapestry needle size 24

EMBROIDERY

Following the graph, embroider the chicken motifs in cross stitch. Work each cross over one fabric square, using three strands of embroidery cotton. Start the embroidery with the centre chicken, 3 cm from the lower edge, matching 'M' with the centre of the fabric. Work a total of seven chickens. Work a row of crosses 3 cm from the top edge, leaving a space of two fabric squares between each cross. When all cross stitching is complete, work the outlines in back stitch, using two strands of cotton.

TO FINISH

Sew the embroidered and cotton pieces together with right sides facing, using 1 cm wide seams, leaving a small opening in the centre of one side. Cut away seam corners diagonally. Turn the placemat right side out, and sew the opening closed.

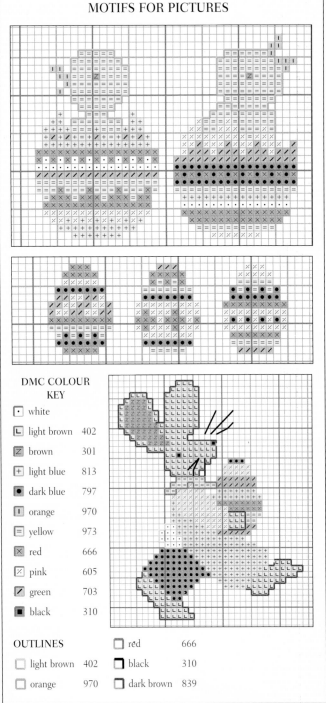

MOTIFS FOR PICTURES

DMC COLOUR KEY

⊡	white	
L	light brown	402
Z	brown	301
+	light blue	813
●	dark blue	797
I	orange	970
=	yellow	973
✕	red	666
⊠	pink	605
✓	green	703
■	black	310

OUTLINES

□	light brown	402	□	red	666
□	orange	970	■	black	310
			□	dark brown	839

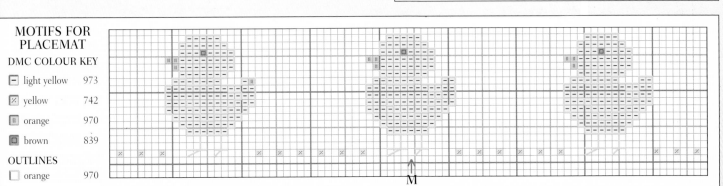

MOTIFS FOR PLACEMAT
DMC COLOUR KEY

−	light yellow	973
⊠	yellow	742
‖	orange	970
⊡	brown	839

OUTLINES

□	orange	970

M

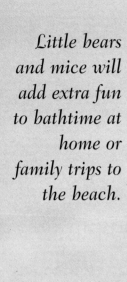

Little bears and mice will add extra fun to bathtime at home or family trips to the beach.

In the swim

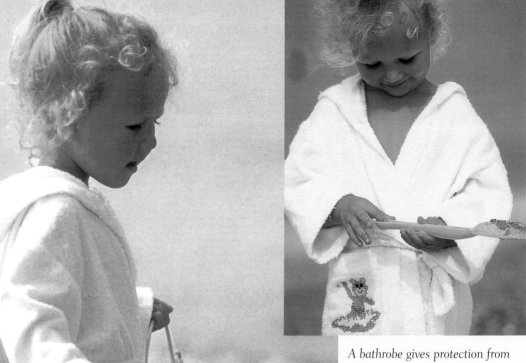

A bathrobe gives protection from the sun and this happy, splashing bear will add to the pleasure of wearing it.

BATHROBE POCKET

Size Pocket about 15 cm square

MATERIALS

Towelling bathrobe with pocket, or use about 20 cm matching towelling fabric if bathrobe has no pocket

12 cm square piece of 10-count waste canvas (ten stitches to 2.5 cm)

DMC stranded embroidery cottons in the colours of the colour key

Crewel needle size 8

Blue hardanger band is the perfect background for this jolly seaside scene—just right to decorate a towel. The instructions are on page 30.

EMBROIDERY

If desired, unpick pocket from bathrobe. Baste the canvas on the right side of the pocket or towelling fabric over the area to be embroidered. Following the graph, embroider the bear motif in cross stitch: position it in the centre, and about 4 cm from the lower raw edge of the pocket. Work each cross through both layers over two canvas threads, using four strands of cotton. Keep the needle perpendicular to the canvas while working, and stitch only through the canvas holes, not the canvas threads. When the cross stitching is complete, work the outlines in back stitch using two strands of black cotton for the mouth, and red (666) for the sunglasses. When the stitching is completed, dampen the canvas and remove the basting and canvas threads one by one with tweezers.

TO FINISH

Fold under the edges of the pocket and stitch it back onto the bathrobe.

BEAR MOTIF FOR TOWEL

DMC COLOUR KEY (also for graph on page 30)			
■ black	310	V dark green	701
Z bright red	606	● blue	797
· white		O turquoise	996
‖ light pink	353	∩ light blue	519
N beige	422	I yellow	444
L light beige	739	**OUTLINES**	
▼ copper	918	☐ black	310
∕ light brown	3064	☐ bright red	606
		☐ beige	422
		☐ white	

TOWEL BORDER

Size Width of border 6 cm

MATERIALS

6 cm wide blue hardanger band with ten double fabric threads per 1 cm, as wide as the towel plus 5 cm for hems

DMC stranded embroidery cottons in the colours of the selected motifs
(see key on page 29)

Tapestry needle size 24
Bathtowel

EMBROIDERY

Following the graphs, embroider the desired motifs in the centre of the band. Work in cross stitch over two double fabric threads, using three strands of embroidery cotton. Place the motifs as desired, or refer to the photograph. When all cross stitching is complete, work the outlines in back stitch, using two strands of cotton: use black (310) for the whiskers, mouths and floating ring and work all other outlines in the same colour as the adjacent crosses.

TO FINISH

Turn short ends to wrong side, and stitch the band in position. Add running stitch over the machine stitches, over two double fabric threads, using two strands of bright red (606).

MOTIFS FOR TOWEL (key on page 29)

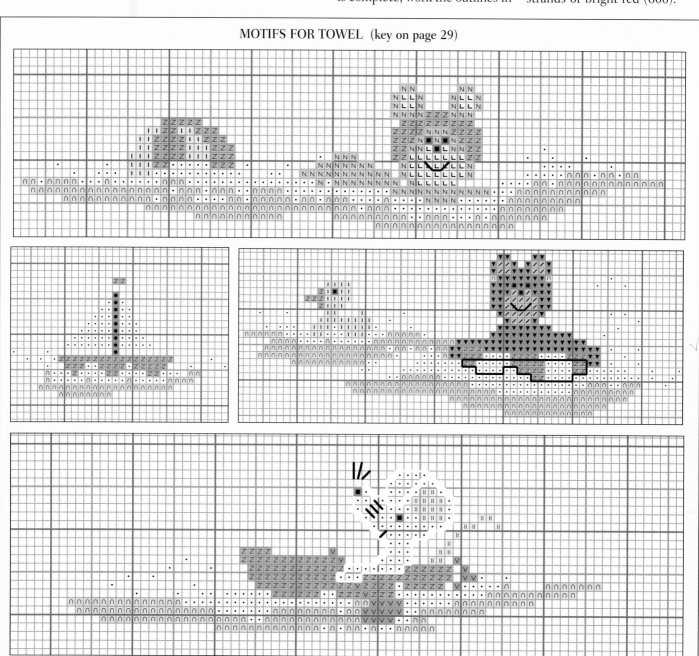

Wildflower magic

Size About 4 x 3.5 cm; motif about 3 x 2.75 cm wide

MATERIALS

8 cm square piece of white 18-count Aida fabric

DMC stranded embroidery cottons in the colours indicated on the colour key

Tapestry needle size 26

4 x 3.5 cm piece of firm white cardboard

6 x 5.5 cm piece of white cotton fabric for the back

Brooch pin

EMBROIDERY

Following the graph, embroider the motif in the centre of the Aida fabric. Work in cross stitch over one fabric square, using two strands of the indicated embroidery cotton.

ASSEMBLY

Cut the completed piece twelve fabric squares outside the embroidery. Stretch it around the cardboard, securing the fabric with large stitches across the back. Stitch the brooch pin to the centre of the cotton fabric. Turn the raw edges 1 cm under, and stitch the cotton fabric against the back of the brooch, with the pin on the outside.

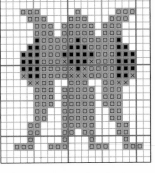

STURT'S DESERT PEA MOTIF FOR BROOCH

DMC COLOUR KEY

▥	red	321
☒	dark red	814
◼	black	310

Give an unusual touch to the plainest white blouse with a lovely stylised flower brooch. It's quick and easy to make.

Welcome baby

This sweet little toy duck makes a delightful card to congratulate the new parents.

Celebrate baby's arrival with a delightful cross-stitched card. And for that special touch, add a miniature scented sachet.

CARD WITH TOY DUCK

Size 15 cm square

MATERIALS

10 cm square piece of white 11-count Aida fabric

Small quantities DMC stranded embroidery cottons in the colours indicated on the colour key

Tapestry needle size 24

15 x 30 cm piece of strong cardboard

15 cm square piece of thin white paper

Small knife or craft knife

Craft glue

EMBROIDERY

Following the graph, embroider the toy duck in the centre of the Aida fabric. Work in cross stitch over one Aida square, using three strands of embroidery cotton. When completed, work the outline (string) in back stitch, using three strands of blue (799). Using red (606) and running stitch, embroider a 5.5 cm square frame around the motif: ensure that the motif is exactly in the centre.

TO ASSEMBLE

Using a small knife, score across the centre of the card to fold it in half. Cut a 6 cm square window in the centre of the front of the card. Centring the motif, glue the embroidered piece behind the window and glue white paper to the inside of the card to cover back of the embroidery.

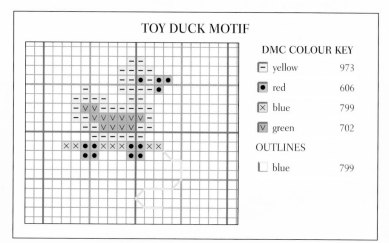

TOY DUCK MOTIF

DMC COLOUR KEY

⊟	yellow	973
⊙	red	606
⊠	blue	799
⊻	green	702

OUTLINES

⌐	blue	799

CARD WITH CRADLE

Size 14 cm square; the motif measures about 5 x 6 cm

MATERIALS

10 cm square piece of white linen with eleven threads per 1 cm or 14-count Aida fabric

DMC stranded embroidery cottons in the colours indicated on the colour key

Tapestry needle size 24

14 x 28 cm piece of thin cardboard or strong paper

13 cm square piece of thin white paper

Small piece of narrow ribbon

Craft glue

EMBROIDERY

Following the graph, embroider the motif in cross stitch in the centre of the linen or Aida fabric. Work each cross over two

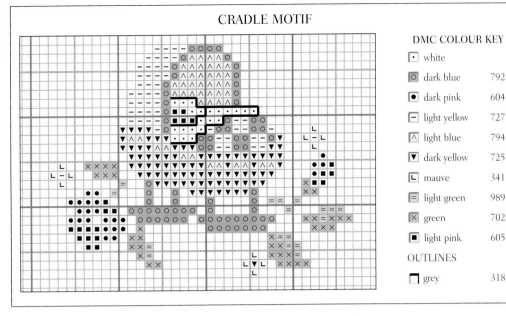

CRADLE MOTIF

DMC COLOUR KEY		
white		
dark blue		792
dark pink		604
light yellow		727
light blue		794
dark yellow		725
mauve		341
light green		989
green		702
light pink		605
OUTLINES		
grey		318

fabric threads or one Aida square, using two strands of embroidery cotton. When all cross stitching is complete, work the outlines in back stitch, using one strand of grey (318). Tie the ribbon into a small bow and sew in place (or glue the ribbon in place after the card has been assembled).

TO ASSEMBLE

Using a small knife, score across the centre of the cardboard on the right side, and fold it double. Cut out a 7 cm square window on the front of the card. Glue the embroidery against the back of the window. Glue white paper to the inside of the card to cover the back of the embroidery.

This pretty card with cradle can be used for congratulations or to announce the birth.

MINIATURE SCENTED SACHETS

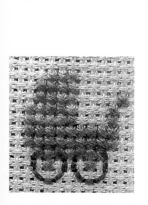

Stitch a tiny scented sachet to pop among baby's clothes.

Size About 11 x 5 cm

MATERIALS

For one bag

30 cm of 5 cm wide self-edged white Aida band with six squares per 1 cm

DMC stranded embroidery cottons in the colours of the selected motif

Tapestry needle size 24

25 cm of 3 mm wide ribbon

Dried lavender or other pot pourri

EMBROIDERY

Fold the band in half to form a bag, and fingerpress the fold. Open the band out again. Following the chosen graph, embroider the motif in the centre of the front of the band, about seven fabric squares above the fold. Work in cross stitch over one fabric square, using two strands of embroidery cotton. When all cross stitching is complete, work the outlines in back stitch, using two strands of cotton. If using the pram motif, work the wheels in dark blue (797); if using the duck motif work the string in blue (799). Press the completed embroidery from the back under a damp cloth.

TO ASSEMBLE

Turn the short ends of the embroidered band about 4 cm inwards, and fold the piece double with wrong sides facing. Using white sewing thread, sew the side edges closely inside the self-edged border. Fill the bag three-quarters full with lavender or pot pourri. Knot ribbon around the bag, about 3 cm from the top edge, and tie it into a bow.

PRAM MOTIF

DMC COLOUR KEY

⊙	light pink	3609
●	dark pink	3608
☒	blue	799
☐	dark blue	797

At a card party—
or just a gathering
of friends—these
coasters decorated
with hearts,
clubs, diamonds
and spades
will certainly be
admired.

Card party

Size 9 cm diameter

MATERIALS

For one coaster

12 cm square piece of white
14-count Aida fabric

12 cm square piece of white
cotton lining fabric

35 cm pale grey bias binding

DMC stranded embroidery
cottons in red (666) or
black (310)

Tapestry needle size 24

METHOD

Outline a 9 cm diameter circle
on the Aida fabric in running
stitch. Fold the circle in four and
press in the creases. Embroider
one motif centred over each fold,
placing the hearts 7 squares out
from the centre square and the
other motifs 5 squares out. When
completed, cut the embroidered
circle on the marked line.

Cut the lining fabric the
same shape as the embroidered
piece. Place the two pieces
together with the wrong sides
facing, and finish by sewing
around the edge with bias
binding.

*Anyone who enjoys
a game of cards
would welcome
a gift of these
coasters.*

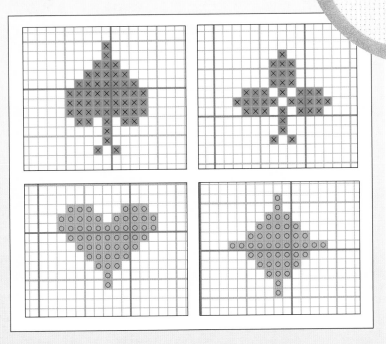

GRAPHS FOR
COASTERS

DMC COLOUR
KEY

⊙	red	666
✕	black	310

35

Always useful, these lovely doorstoppers with flower motifs are decorative as well. Choose from a round one filled with pebbles or a covered brick.

Open sesame

A magnificent cross-stitched waterlily makes this covered brick a work of art.

MOTIF FOR WATERLILY

DMC COLOUR KEY

∩	yellow-green	907
H	dark green	699
▣	light green	702
I	blue-green	913
↓	light pink	605
◹	medium pink	604
∅	dark pink	603
▶	yellow	307
◥	orange	742
∨	brown	3032
✕	grey	414

OUTLINES

▢	very dark green	895
▢	very dark pink	601

DOORBRICK WITH WATERLILY

Size Covered brick 23 x 11.5 x 7.5 cm

MATERIALS

40 cm square piece of decorative strong fabric

About 15 x 20 cm piece of white 14-count Aida fabric

DMC stranded embroidery cottons in the colours indicated on the colour key

Tapestry needle size 24

60 cm of 5 mm wide decorative pink braid

About 15 x 10 cm piece of fusible webbing

Polyester batting to pad brick

Completely dry common house brick (It is a good idea to keep the brick inside for at least two weeks before assembling the doorstop, or bake it in the oven to be sure it is dry.)

EMBROIDERY

Following the graph, embroider the waterlily in the centre of the Aida fabric. When all cross stitching is complete, work the outlines in back stitch, using one strand of cotton. When stitching is completed, iron fusible webbing to the back of the embroidery, and cut the piece so that it measures 14 x 9 cm, with the motif in the centre.

TO ASSEMBLE

Cover the brick evenly with a layer of batting. Measure the brick accurately and, following the diagram, make a paper pattern for the cover (alter the given measurements of the diagram if necessary). Cut out the fabric piece, adding 1 cm seam allowances all around. Sew the short side seams together, with right sides facing, making 1 cm wide seams. Turn right side out. Place the brick inside the cover. Fold in the 1 cm seam allowances, and handsew the remaining sides of the cover closed (i.e. one long and two short sides, forming the base of the cover).

Remove the paper layer from the fusible webbing, and use it when ironing the embroidered piece in the centre of the top of the cover. Glue or sew braid around the outer edges of the embroidered piece to cover the edges and protect them from fraying.

PATTERN FOR BRICK COVER

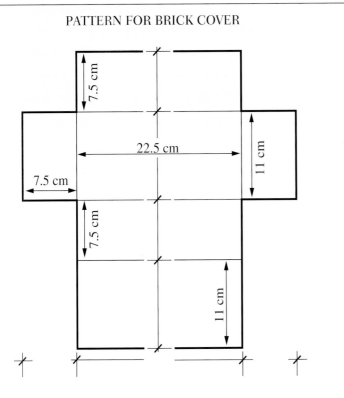

7.5 cm

22.5 cm

7.5 cm

11 cm

7.5 cm

11 cm

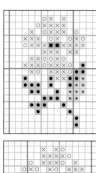

MOTIFS FOR YELLOW FLOWERS

DMC COLOUR KEY

☒	dark yellow	972
⦿	dark green	701
⊙	light yellow	307
✳	light green	907
■	dark red	902

DOORSTOPPER WITH YELLOW FLOWERS

Size 18 cm diameter; flower motif about 3 cm square

MATERIALS

25 cm square piece of medium blue 14-count Aida fabric

DMC stranded embroidery cottons in the colours indicated on the colour key

Tapestry needle size 24

25 cm square piece of strong dark blue fabric for the back

22 x 44 cm piece of closely woven fabric for the insert

Prewashed small aquarium stones, thoroughly dried

60 cm of 1 cm wide decorative yellow braid

EMBROIDERY

Make a paper pattern of an 18 cm diameter circle. Use running stitches to outline the pattern on the Aida fabric. Following the two graphs of the motif (one is reversed), embroider a circle of flowers about 2.5 cm within the marked outline. Use 3 cm square pieces of paper to determine their position. Or, if you prefer, embroider a number of flowers scattered within the marked circle. When completed, cut the Aida fabric 1 cm outside the marked line.

TO ASSEMBLE

Unless otherwise indicated, sew all pieces together with right sides facing, using 1 cm wide seams.

Fold the fabric for the insert double, making it 22 cm square. Place the 18 cm diameter circular pattern on top, and trace around with a soft pencil. Cut out, adding a 1 cm seam allowance. Sew the two pieces together, leaving an opening for turning and filling. Clip seam curves and turn the insert right side out. Fill with stones and sew the opening closed.

Cut the paper pattern in half. Cut both pattern pieces from backing fabric, adding 1 cm seams all around. Sew the two pieces together along the straight sides, leaving a generous opening in the centre for turning and to add the insert. Sew the front and backing together. Clip seam curves, and turn the cover right side out through the back opening.

Place the insert inside the cover, and slipstitch the opening closed. With short ends turned under, sew decorative braid over the seam at the outer edge of the doorstopper.

EXTRA MOTIF — AEROPLANE

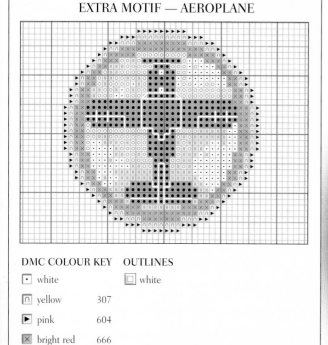

DMC COLOUR KEY   OUTLINES

⊡	white		☐	white
⊓	yellow	307		
▶	pink	604		
☒	bright red	666		
⊙	light pale blue	775		
⦿	very dark blue	796		
‖	light blue	809		

A circle of yellow flowers looks very attractive on the blue Aida fabric of this doorstopper. It makes a lovely giant pincushion, too.

Size About 9 x 18 cm; motif about 5 x 3.5 cm

MATERIALS

25 cm square piece of beige-grey 14-count Aida fabric

DMC stranded embroidery cottons in the colours indicated on the colour key

Tapestry needle size 24

25 cm square piece of matching cotton lining fabric

Heavyweight interfacing

One snap fastener

80 cm of bright blue bias binding

EMBROIDERY

Cut the Aida fabric into two 12.5 x 25 cm pieces. Following the graph, embroider the lorikeet motif on one of the pieces in cross stitch. Work each cross over one fabric square, using two strands of embroidery cotton. Start working with the brown branch, 7 cm from the lower edge and 3.5 cm from the right-hand edge (one long side of the piece).

CUTTING OUT

Enlarge the pattern graph and cut out the pattern. Cut A and B together (forming one piece, the back of the case and the flap) without seam allowance from the plain piece of Aida fabric, the interfacing and the lining fabric. Cut A (one piece without the flap, forming the front of the case) without seam allowance from the embroidered piece: ensure that the motif is positioned in the centre, 4 cm from the lower edge. Cut A once also from the interfacing and once from the lining fabric without seam.

Rainbow hues

Keep your glasses safe in this attractive cross-stitched glasses case. The edges are bound with bias binding.

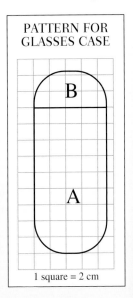

PATTERN FOR GLASSES CASE

B

A

1 square = 2 cm

Rainbow lorikeets make a colourful motif for this practical glasses case.

TO ASSEMBLE

Tack front (A) Aida and lining pieces together with wrong sides facing and the interfacing inserted between. Repeat with the pieces for back of case. Finish straight top edge of front (A) with bias binding. Pin front on top of back with the lining sides facing, and the flap extending. Finish the case all around with bias binding. Sew on the snap fastener to close the flap.

LORIKEET MOTIF

DMC COLOUR KEY

⌒	light green	704
ıı	medium green	702
H	dark green	701
⌐	light blue	798
⊥	dark blue	797
✕	red	666
◇	brown	869
⊼	orange-yellow	741

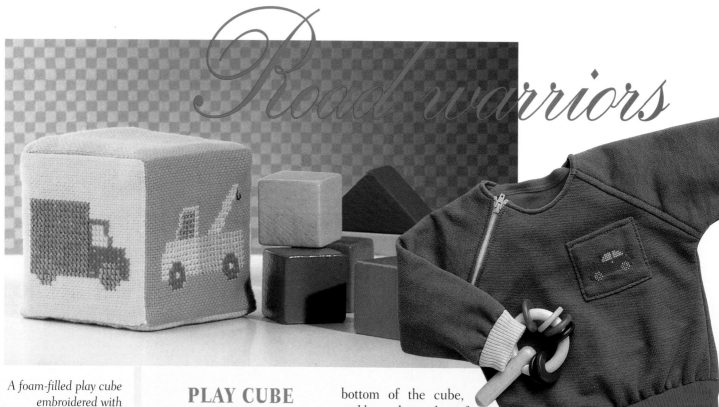

A foam-filled play cube embroidered with trucks and car will give baby hours of pleasure.

Bright colours and simple shapes will amuse your little ones, and they will love these car and truck motifs. Use them on a play cube, pocket, card — or anywhere else you can think of.

PLAY CUBE

Size 7 x 7 x 7 cm

MATERIALS

Two 9 cm square pieces each of light blue, light green and yellow hardanger fabric, with nine double fabric threads per 1 cm

DMC stranded embroidery cottons in the colours indicated on the colour key

Tapestry needle size 24

7 x 7 x 7 cm foam plastic cube

EMBROIDERY

Following the graph, embroider a car or truck in the centre of each of the blue and yellow pieces. Work in cross stitch over two double fabric threads, using three strands of embroidery cotton. When all cross stitching is complete, work the outlines in back stitch, using two strands of cotton in black for the tow-truck, and red for the car.

TO FINISH

Using 1 cm wide seams, sew the six pieces together into a cube: use green pieces for the top and bottom of the cube, and leave three edges of one piece open to insert the filling. Clip seam corners, and turn right side out. Insert the foam cube, and sew the opening closed.

TRACKSUIT POCKET

Size Motif 2.5 x 5 cm

MATERIALS

Tracksuit top or sweatshirt with a pocket

5 x 8 cm piece of 14-count waste canvas (fourteen stitches to 2.5 cm)

DMC stranded embroidery cottons in the colours of car motif

Crewel needle size 8

EMBROIDERY

Remove the pocket from the top. Baste the waste canvas over the area of the pocket to be embroidered: the car should be positioned in the centre, about 2 cm from the lower edge of the finished pocket. Following the graph, embroider the motif through both layers, over two canvas threads, using two strands of embroidery cotton. Keep the needle perpendicular to the canvas while you are working, and stitch only through the canvas holes, not the canvas threads. When completed, dampen the

canvas, and remove the basting and canvas threads one by one with tweezers. Sew the pocket back on the top.

CARD

Size 10.5 x 14.5 cm

MATERIALS

7 cm square piece of white 18-count Aida fabric

DMC stranded embroidery cottons in the colours of the selected motif

Tapestry needle size 26

21 x 14.5 cm piece of blue cardboard or strong paper

7 cm square piece of thin white paper

Craft glue

EMBROIDERY

Following the graph, embroider the selected car or truck in the centre of the fabric. Work in cross stitch over one Aida square, using two strands of embroidery cotton. When completed, work the back stitches for the tow-truck

GRAPH FOR TRUCKS AND CAR

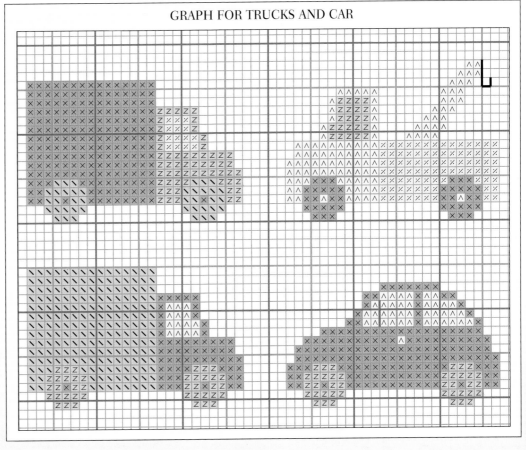

in black, and for the car in red.

TO ASSEMBLE

Using a small knife, score across the centre of the card to fold it double. Cut out a 4 x 5 cm window from the front

of the card. Glue the embroidery against the back of the window, and cover the back of the embroidery with white paper glued in place.

DMC COLOUR KEY

⋀	yellow	726
⊾	blue	334
Z	green	704
⟋	pink	604
✕	red	666

OUTLINES

☐	red	666
☐	black	310

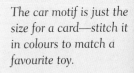

The car motif is just the size for a card—stitch it in colours to match a favourite toy.

Centre: The little red car looks bright and cheery, and it matches the red trim on the tracksuit top.

A scatter of soft pink cherries decorates this lovely cloth. The shape of the cloth and arrangement of the motifs can be adapted to suit any tray shape.

Cherry chip

Size Cloth 35 x 45 cm, motif about 4.5 cm square

MATERIALS

40 x 50 cm piece of white evenweave linen with twelve fabric threads per 1 cm

DMC stranded embroidery cottons in the colours indicated on the colour key

Tapestry needle size 26

The bunches of cherries can be stitched so quickly and yet are very effective.

METHOD

Enlarge the pattern graph and cut out the paper pattern. Pin the pattern on the linen and outline the shape with running stitches. Following the graph, embroider the cherry motifs in cross stitch, staying at least 1.5 cm inside the marked outline. Position the motifs as you prefer, using 4.5 cm paper squares to determine their position. Work each cross over three fabric threads, using two strands of embroidery cotton. Work the outlines in back stitch, using two strands of green (954).

Finish the cloth as desired, by edging with lace or bias binding, or crocheting a simple border all around it.

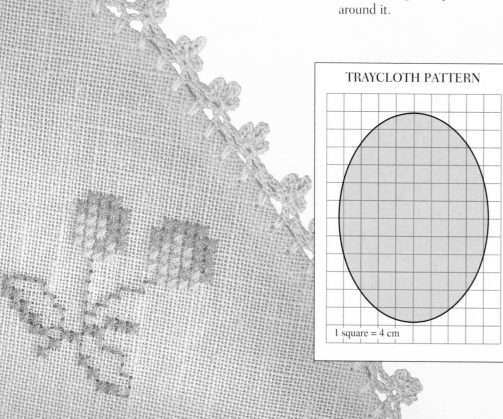

TRAYCLOTH PATTERN

1 square = 4 cm

CHERRY MOTIF

DMC COLOUR KEY

⊙	green	954
⊠	dark pink	962
☑	pink	963

OUTLINES

☐	green	954

Use as many or as few motifs as you like, but space them evenly over the traycloth for the best effect.

Teapot trio

Three exquisitely cross-stitched teapots framed with bright fabric mats and wood make a stylish and modern wall decoration. The motifs could also be used to decorate a traycloth or tablecloth.

Size Motifs about 5.5 x 8 cm, 6 x 8 cm and 7 x 8 cm; frames 24.5 x 25.5 cm

MATERIALS

For three pictures

Three 35 cm square pieces of white evenweave linen with ten threads per 1 cm

DMC stranded embroidery cottons in the colours indicted on the colour key

Tapestry needle size 24

Three different pieces of striped fabric, each about 30 cm square

Fusible webbing

Three white wooden frames

Three mats with inner measurement of 8 x 9 cm

EMBROIDERY

Following the graph, embroider a different teapot motif in the centre of each piece of linen.

Work in cross stitch over two fabric threads, using two strands of embroidery cotton. When all cross stitching is complete, work the outlines in back stitch, using one strand of brown (3032) embroidery cotton.

TO ASSEMBLE

Iron fusible webbing to back of the striped fabrics. On the paper layer of the webbing trace the measurement of the mat, and cut out accurately. Remove the paper layer, and iron the fabric onto the mat. Frame the embroidered piece and mat.

These elegant cross-stitched pictures help to create a contemporary atmosphere. The delicate teapot designs are set off by the striking striped and check fabric mats.

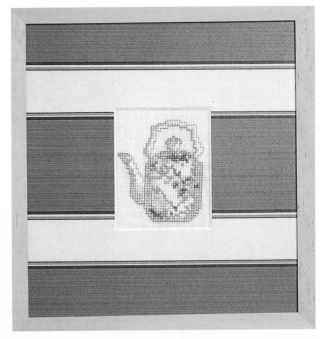

TEAPOT WITH PINK KNOB

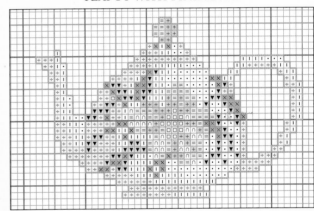

TEAPOT WITH HIGH STAND

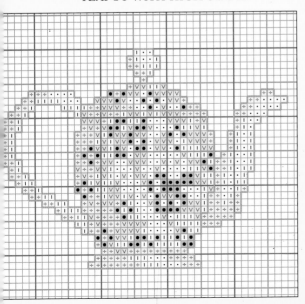

KETTLE TEAPOT

TEAPOT MOTIFS

DMC COLOUR KEY

·	white	
I	ecru	
●	antique rose	223
V	light antique rose	224
◻	yellow-green	472
±	light pink-brown	842
⊠	grey-blue	931
▼	grey-green	3013
L	light green	3348
✕	dark green	3363
⊟	pink	3688
∩	light pink	3689
+	dark pink	3731

OUTLINES

☐	brown	3032

45

Cuddly kittens and lovable dogs can be the most endearing of motifs. Use them where you'll see them every day—the pictures with bright red or blue wooden frames are especially cheerful, or turn the embroidery into a useful paperweight for your desk.

Pet projects

PICTURES WITH KITTENS

Size 11 cm square

MATERIALS

For each picture

16 cm square piece of white 11-count Aida fabric

DMC stranded embroidery cottons in the colours indicated on the colour key for the desired kitten motif

Tapestry needle size 24

Matching wooden frame

EMBROIDERY

Following the graph, embroider the motif in the centre of the Aida fabric. Work in cross stitch over one fabric square, using three strands of embroidery cotton. When all cross stitching is complete, work the outlines in back stitch, using two strands of cotton: use grey (414) for the black kitten, black for the grey kitten and dark brown (300) for the ginger kitten. Work the mouths in black cotton.

TO FINISH

Frame the completed embroidery yourself or have it framed.

PAPERWEIGHT WITH SCOTTIE

Size 9 cm diameter; motif 4.5 x 3.25 cm

MATERIALS

9 cm diameter showcase paperweight

15 cm square piece of white 18-count Aida fabric

DMC stranded embroidery cottons in the colours indicated on the colour key

Tapestry needle size 26

10 cm square piece of iron-on interfacing

EMBROIDERY

Following the graph, embroider the motif in the centre of the fabric. Work in cross stitch over one fabric square, using two strands of embroidery cotton. When all cross stitching is completed, outline the single black cross stitch of the eye in back stitch, using one strand of white.

TO ASSEMBLE

With centres matched, iron interfacing to the back of the embroidered piece. Trim to fit, and place it inside paper weight. Assemble the paperweight as instructed on the packaging.

A paperweight is always handy and can be the perfect gift for someone who has everything, especially when decorated with this fine scottie dog.

MOTIF FOR SCOTTIE PAPERWEIGHT

DMC COLOUR KEY

■	black	310
●	dark grey	413
◎	light grey	414
✕	red	666

OUTLINES

∟	white	

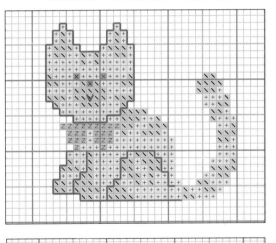

DMC COLOUR KEY

∨	grey	414
−	light grey	415
✕	black	310
·	ecru	746
●	red	666
+	orange	741
z	blue	995
⊼	brown	921
∩	green	702

OUTLINES

☐	light grey	415
◪	black	310
◪	dark brown	300

MOTIFS FOR KITTEN PICTURES

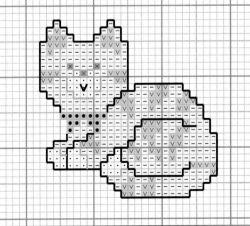

Above: Touches of red contrast with black and grey kittens for a young, modern look.

Left: Blue accents complement bright contemporary decor but will fit equally well into a more traditional setting.

Pink and pretty

Give yourself a treat by making these matching compact, comb and mirror cases with their delightful and colourful galah motifs. They'll also make very lovely gifts.

Subtle tones of pink and grey make a very pleasing combination on this matching set of compact, mirror and comb cases.

COMPACT CASE

Size About 9 cm in diameter; motif 4.75 x 3.5 cm (If necessary, adapt measurements of case for a different sized compact.)

MATERIALS

30 x 15 cm piece of pale pink 14-count Aida fabric

24 x 12 cm piece of flowered cotton lining fabric

24 x 12 cm piece of heavy-weight interfacing

DMC stranded embroidery cottons in the colours indicated on the colour key

Tapestry needle size 24

EMBROIDERY

Cut the Aida fabric in half to obtain two 15 x 15 cm square pieces. Using running stitch, outline a 9 cm diameter circle on one piece of the fabric. Following the graph, embroider the galah motif in the centre of the marked circle. Work in cross stitch over one fabric square, using two strands of embroidery cotton. When the embroidery is completed, cut the outlined circle 1 cm from the marked line.

TO ASSEMBLE

Cut five 11 cm diameter circles, one from remaining Aida fabric, two from lining fabric and two from interfacing.

Baste the interfacing to the back of the two Aida circles. Using 1 cm wide seam, sew a lining and a reinforced piece together with right sides facing, leaving a small opening for

turning. Trim and clip the seams. Repeat with remaining pieces. Turn each piece right side out and slip stitch the opening closed. Baste and hand sew the two circles together with the lined sides facing, leaving the top edge about one quarter open to insert the compact. Decorate the edges with blanket stitch, using two strands of pink (961) embroidery cotton.

COMB CASE

Size About 5 x 14 cm, motif about 2.5 x 3.5 cm (If necessary, adapt the measurements of the case for a different sized comb.)

MATERIALS

15 x 20 cm piece of pale pink 14-count Aida fabric

15 x 20 cm piece of flowered cotton lining fabric

30 cm piece of pale grey bias binding

DMC stranded embroidery cottons in colours indicated on colour key, but omit green (368)

Tapestry needle size 24

EMBROIDERY

Make a paper pattern and, using running stitches, outline the pattern on the Aida fabric. Following the graph, embroider the galah motif on the front section of the case. Work in cross stitch over one fabric square, using two strands of embroidery cotton. Position the motif 2 cm from the lower marked edge, and 1.25 cm from the right-hand marked edge. Omit the three bottom stitches of the brown branch and also the green leaf (refer to the photograph). When the embroidery is completed, cut out the embroidered piece on the marked lines.

To ASSEMBLE

Place the lining and Aida pieces together with wrong sides facing. Finish the straight top edge with bias binding. Fold the case in half, with the lining sides facing. Finish the outer edge of the case with bias binding.

MIRROR CASE

Size About 9 x 7 cm, motif 4.75 x 3.5 cm (If necessary, adapt the measurements of the case for a different sized mirror.)

MATERIALS

18 x 9 cm piece of pale pink 14-count Aida fabric

18 x 9 cm piece of strong lining fabric

DMC stranded embroidery cottons in the colours indicated on the colour key

Tapestry needle size 24

15 cm pale grey bias binding

8 x 6 cm mirror

METHOD

Work overcast stitches all around the Aida fabric to prevent the edges from unravelling. Fold the Aida fabric double, making it 9 x 9 cm, and finger-press the fold. Fold the fabric open again. Following the graph, embroider the motif in the centre of the fabric, about 1 cm upwards from the crease. Work in cross stitch over one fabric square, using two strands of embroidery cotton.

To ASSEMBLE

Place the lining and embroidered pieces together with wrong sides facing. Finish both short ends with bias binding. Fold the piece double, with the Aida sides facing. Sew the side edges using 1 cm wide seams. Trim and tidy the seams with zig-zag stitching. Turn the cover right side out.

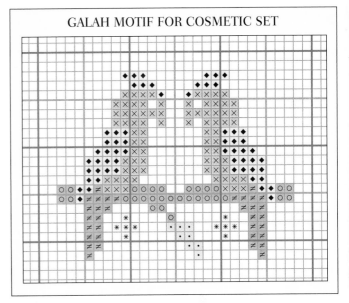

GALAH MOTIF FOR COSMETIC SET

DMC COLOUR KEY

◆	light grey	415
✕	pink	961
○	brown	841
✳	blue	827
•	green	368
⇄	dark grey	414

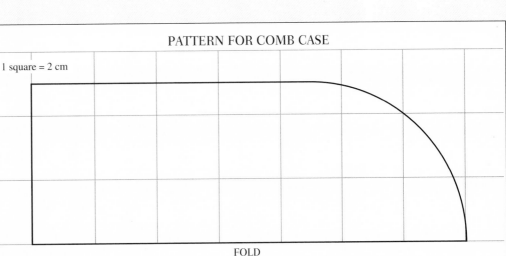

PATTERN FOR COMB CASE

1 square = 2 cm

FOLD

PINK AND PRETTY

Sheer simplicity

When you want to give
more than a thought, a
handkerchief with
cross-stitched motif is
an ideal gift.

Beautiful and
practical, too.
Turn a simple
handkerchief
into something
special by
embroidering an
initial or rosebud
in one corner.

MATERIALS

Handkerchief

Small piece of 14-count waste
canvas

Small quantities DMC
stranded embroidery
cottons in the colours
of the required rosebud
or initial
(The illustrated
initials are worked in grey
415 and light blue 827)

Crewel needle size 8

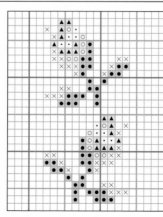

ROSEBUD MOTIFS

DMC COLOUR KEY

⊡ light pink 818 or light yellow 745

◯ medium pink 3708 or
   medium yellow 743

▲ dark pink 3706 or
   dark yellow 742

☒ green 369 or green 368

⬤ dark green 989 or dark green 367

50

METHOD

Baste the waste canvas on the right side of a handkerchief, in one corner. Following the graph, embroider motif through both layers in cross stitch. Work each cross over two canvas threads, using two strands of embroidery cotton. Keep needle perpendicular to canvas while working, and stitch only through canvas holes, not the canvas threads. When completed, dampen the canvas, and remove the basting and canvas threads one by one with tweezers. Iron the handkerchief from the back, using a damp cloth.

ALPHABET FOR HANDKERCHIEFS

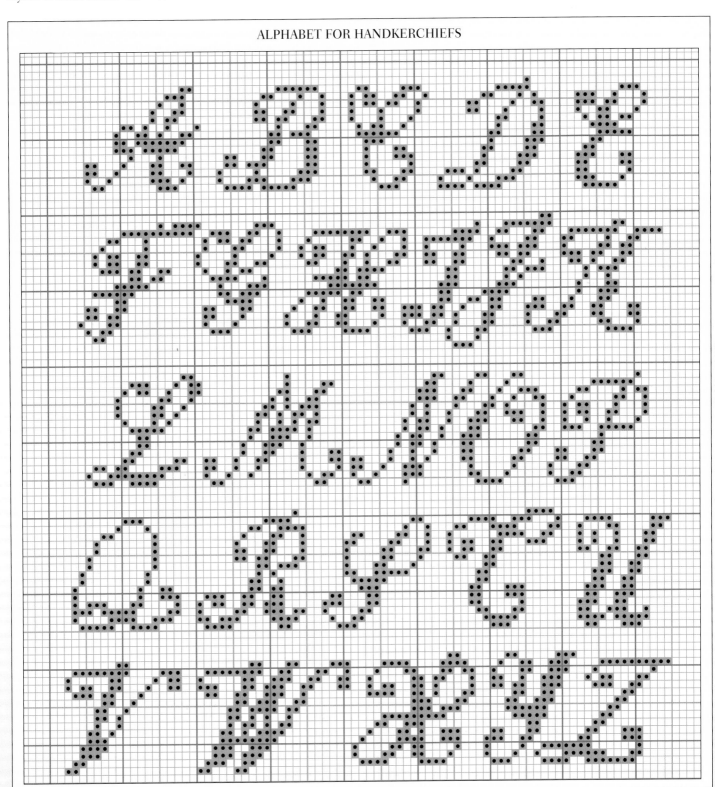

Join the parade

When making a dress or romper suit, substitute Aida fabric for the yoke and embroider these bright and cheerful little figures. They could also be put together to make a picture of the parade, or used on a very special birthday card.

Size Embroidery about 8 x 5 cm

MATERIALS

Piece of white 18-count Aida fabric

DMC stranded embroidery cottons in the colours indicated on the colour key

Tapestry needle size 26

EMBROIDERY

Following the graph, embroider the motif in cross stitch in the centre of the Aida fabric. Work each cross over one fabric square using two strands of embroidery cotton.

Baby will love an outfit embroidered with colourful little musicians.

The finishing touch for these outfits is an embroidered panel, with three little girls bedecked with flowers or a cheerful band.

MOTIF OF THREE GIRLS

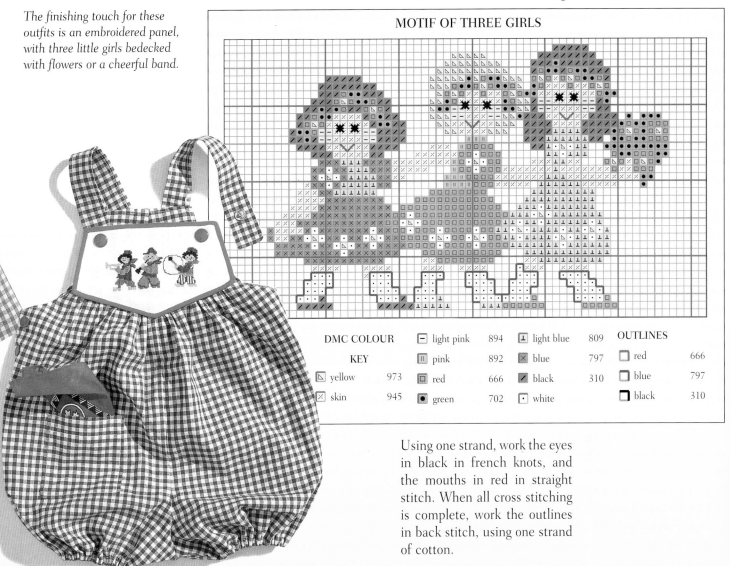

DMC COLOUR						OUTLINES	
KEY		⊟ light pink	894	⊥ light blue	809	□ red	666
◿ yellow	973	‖ pink	892	⊠ blue	797	□ blue	797
⊠ skin	945	▦ red	666	◢ black	310	□ black	310
		● green	702	· white			

Using one strand, work the eyes in black in french knots, and the mouths in red in straight stitch. When all cross stitching is complete, work the outlines in back stitch, using one strand of cotton.

MOTIF OF BOY MUSICIANS

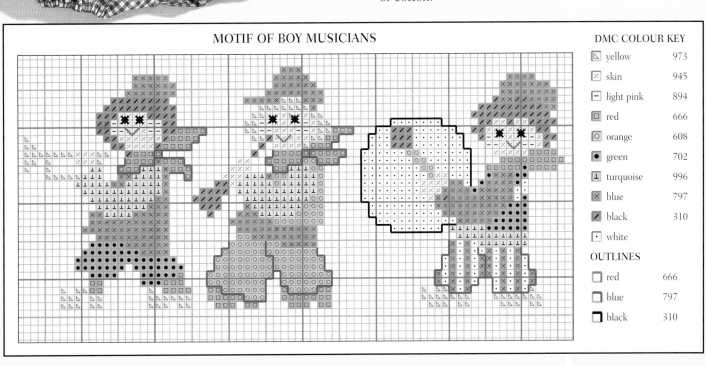

DMC COLOUR KEY	
◿ yellow	973
⊠ skin	945
⊟ light pink	894
▦ red	666
◎ orange	608
● green	702
⊥ turquoise	996
⊠ blue	797
◢ black	310
· white	
OUTLINES	
□ red	666
□ blue	797
□ black	310

An initial on an album or notebook cover is much more attractive than a written label.

Initial touch

Add a romantic touch to gifts for young or old by cross stitching an initial in flowing script. Soft, pastel colours will enhance the theme.

ALBUM COVER

Size The illustrated cover is for an album 21 cm square, with a 2 cm wide spine (If necessary, adapt the measurements of the cover for a differently sized album.)

MATERIALS

25 x 60 cm piece of pink-white checked or white Aida fabric

25 x 60 cm piece each of white cotton for lining and thin batting

DMC stranded embroidery cotton in pink (3708)

Tapestry needle size 24

EMBROIDERY

Following the alphabet graph, embroider the required letter on the Aida fabric in cross stitch. Work each cross over two fabric squares, using three strands of embroidery cotton. (The lines of the woven check are two fabric squares wide and three fabric squares long: simply embroider over the lines.) Position the letter in the centre of the front of the cover, allowing for the side flaps.

TO FINISH

Place the Aida and cotton pieces together with right sides facing, and place the batting on top. Sew together with 2 cm wide seam, leaving an opening for turning on one short side. Cut away seam corners diagonally, and trim the seams. Turn the cover right side out, and sew the opening closed. Fold the sides 6 cm inwards, and secure them along both the top and bottom edges. Place the album inside the cover.

WASHMITTEN

Size Initial measures about 4.5 x 6 cm

MATERIALS

White washmitten or washer

About 7 x 9 cm piece of 10-count waste canvas (ten stitches to 2.5 cm)

DMC stranded embroidery cotton in pink (3708)

Crewel needle size 8

EMBROIDERY

Baste the waste canvas over the centre of the washmitten or corner of a washer. Following the alphabet graph, embroider the required letter in cross stitch. Work each cross through both layers over two canvas threads, using three strands of embroidery cotton. Keep the needle perpendicular to the canvas while working, and stitch only through the canvas holes, not the canvas threads. When completed, dampen the canvas, and remove the basting and canvas threads one by one with tweezers. If preferred, work a border in satin stitch over the self-woven border.

A personalised washmitten is hygienic as well as pretty.

MAKING A WASHMITTEN

To make a washmitten, fold a washer in half and stitch the side and bottom seams closed. Turn the washmitten right side out and flatten out the seams.

ALPHABET FOR ALBUM COVER AND WASHMITTEN

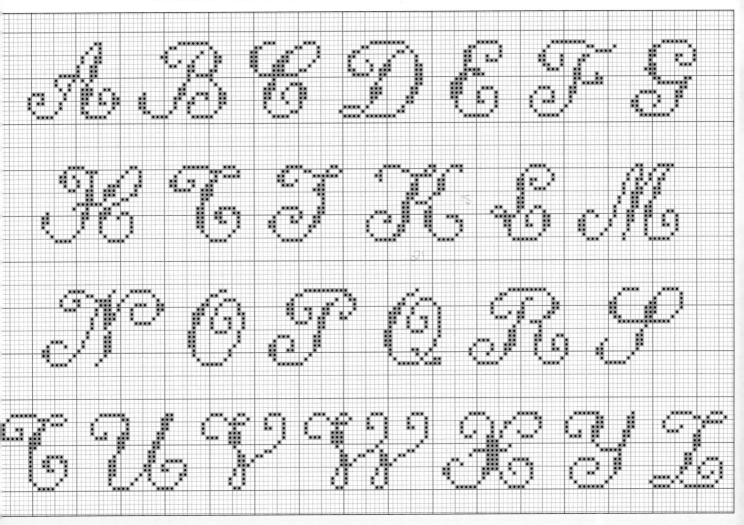

Miniature beauties

Quick to make and beautiful to look at, these tiny pictures will be a constant delight. Stand them on a mantlepiece or occasional table, or hang them singly or in groups for stunning effect.

EMUS MAKING TRACKS

Size Outer edge of frame 9 x 6.5 cm; motif 5.5 x 3 cm

MATERIALS

12 x 10 cm piece of white 18-count Aida fabric

DMC stranded embroidery cottons in the colours indicated on the colour key

Tapestry needle size 26

10 cm square piece of iron-on interfacing

Brown frame with outer edge measuring 9 x 6.5 cm

METHOD

Following the graph, embroider the motif in the centre of the fabric. Work in cross stitch over one fabric square, using two strands of cotton. When it is completed, iron interfacing to the back of the piece, with centres matched. Cut the piece to measure a little less than 9 x 6.5 cm, with the motif in the centre. Place it inside the frame.

BLUEBIRD OF HAPPINESS

Size Picture 6 cm diameter; motif 4 x 3.25 cm

MATERIALS

10 cm square piece of white 18-count Aida fabric

DMC stranded embroidery cottons in the colours on the colour key (page 58)

Tapestry needle size 26

8 cm square piece of iron-on interfacing

6 cm diameter circular gold frame

MOTIF FOR EMU PICTURE

| DMC COLOUR KEY | ▣ dark gold | 920 |
| ⊠ gold | 976 | Ⅰ purple | 208 |

Use a favourite motif to make a miniature picture and put it where you'll see it often. There's a motif here for everyone — and a frame to suit each motif.

MOTIF FOR BLUEBIRD

DMC COLOUR KEY

- ⊡ light blue   800
- ● dark blue   797
- ⊙ medium blue   798
- ⊠ turquoise   996

MOTIF FOR FLOWER BASKET

DMC COLOUR KEY

⊠ pink	776	◣ light gold	783	⊡ dark green	562
⊟ bright red	349	＋ dark gold	780	⊟ light blue	800
● dark red	816	s light green	955	⊡ dark blue	799

METHOD

Work as described for the emu picture, but cut the reinforced piece into a 6 cm diameter circle, with the motif in the centre.

BUTTERFLY

Size Frame 9 x 6.5 cm; motif 6 x 4 cm

MATERIALS

12 x 10 cm piece of white 14-count Aida fabric

DMC stranded embroidery cottons in the colours of the blue-purple butterfly motif on page 68

Tapestry needle size 24

Pewter frame with stand

METHOD

Following the graph for the hanging sachet on page 68, embroider the motif in cross stitch in the centre of the Aida fabric. Work each cross over one Aida square, using two strands of embroidery cotton. When all cross stitching is complete, work the outlines in back stitch, using one strand of cotton in the darkest shade of adjacent crosses. Frame in the same way as for the emu picture (page 56).

FLOWER BASKET

Size Outer measurements of picture 15 cm square; motif 8 x 7.5 cm

MATERIALS

20 cm square piece of white 14-count Aida fabric

DMC stranded embroidery cottons in the colours indicated on the colour key

Tapestry needle size 24

White plastic frame, 15 cm square

EMBROIDERY

Work as for the emu picture, but cut the piece to a little less than 15 cm square.

Cornflower blue

This beautiful keyring attachment can be stitched in an evening for years of pleasure.

Size 4 cm diameter; motif about 2 cm square

MATERIALS

38 mm diameter blue plastic needlework frame

10 cm square piece of white 18-count Aida fabric

DMC stranded embroidery cottons in the colours indicated on the colour key

Tapestry needle size 26

Steel clip section of a keyring (or you can attach the embroidered frame to your existing keyring)

Small piece of strong wire and a pair of pliers

Craft glue

EMBROIDERY

Following the graph, embroider the flower motif in the centre of the fabric in cross stitch. Work each cross over one fabric square, using two strands of embroidery cotton. When completed, work the outlines in back stitch, using one strand in dark blue (792).

TO ASSEMBLE

Trace the cardboard circle of the frame onto the embroidered fabric, ensuring that the motif is exactly in the centre. Cut out. Apply small dots of glue around the outside edge of the cardboard circle. Place the embroidery inside the frame, and press the cardboard circle inside the frame, against the back of the embroidery. Leave to dry. Using the piece of wire and pliers, attach the steel section of the keyring through the hanger of the frame. Press the ends of the wire securely together, forming a circle. Or add the frame, through the hanger, to your existing keyring.

The intense blue of the flower is reflected in the colour of the tiny embroidery frame.

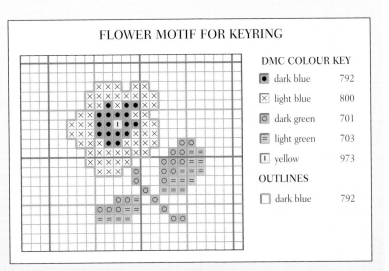

FLOWER MOTIF FOR KEYRING

DMC COLOUR KEY

●	dark blue	792
☒	light blue	800
◎	dark green	701
≡	light green	703
I	yellow	973

OUTLINES

☐	dark blue	792

Turn a plain blouse into a work of art with an embroidered pocket. You'll be the envy of all your friends.

DMC COLOUR KEY

●	dark salmon pink	350
○	salmon pink	352
■	grey	413
▲	brown	434
T	moss-green	469
\	very light green	472
U	medium green	701
−	yellow	727
⊠	light brown	834
L	green	989
I	light green	3348
✳	very light salmon pink	3770

OUTLINES

▢	dark green	699

Pretty pockets

Bird-lovers will be delighted with these attractive budgies.

MOTIF FOR APPLE

APPLE

Size Motif about 8.5 x 9.5 cm

MATERIALS

White blouse with breast pocket

DMC stranded embroidery cottons in the colours indicated on the colour key

Crewel needle size 8

12 cm square piece of 10-count waste canvas (ten stitches to 2.5 cm)

METHOD

Carefully unpick the pocket from the blouse. Baste the waste canvas on the right side of the pocket over the area to be embroidered. Following the graph, embroider the motif in cross stitch in the centre of the pocket, about 1.5 cm from the lower edge. Work each cross through both layers over two canvas threads, using three strands of embroidery cotton. Keep the needle perpendicular to the canvas while working, and stitch only through the canvas holes, not the canvas threads.

60

When all cross stitching is complete, work the outlines in back stitch, using two strands of dark green (699). When completed, dampen the canvas, and remove the basting and canvas threads one by one with tweezers. Sew the pocket back onto the blouse.

BUDGIES IN LOVE

Size Motif about 10 x 10 cm

MATERIALS

White blouse with a pocket of linen with 11 threads to 1 cm (or use 17.5 x 16.5 cm piece of 14-count Aida fabric as a pocket)

DMC stranded embroidery cottons in the colours indicated on the colour key

Tapestry needle size 24

METHOD

Unpick the pocket. Following the graph, embroider the motif in cross stitch on the pocket or Aida fabric. Work each cross over two linen threads (or one Aida fabric square), using two strands of embroidery cotton. When all cross stitching is complete, work the outlines in back stitch using one strand of cotton: work the head of the left-hand budgie in blue (799) and the breast in bright green (907); the outline of the right-hand budgie in orange (741); the outline of the beaks, the eyes and the branch in brown (420) and/or dark brown (839), as preferred.

Sew the pocket back onto the blouse, over the old seam line.

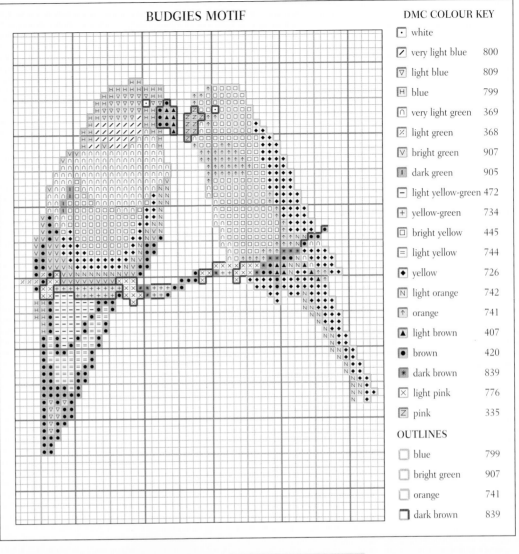

BUDGIES MOTIF

DMC COLOUR KEY

·	white	
✓	very light blue	800
▽	light blue	809
H	blue	799
∩	very light green	369
⊠	light green	368
∨	bright green	907
∎	dark green	905
−	light yellow-green	472
+	yellow-green	734
▢	bright yellow	445
⊟	light yellow	744
◆	yellow	726
N	light orange	742
↑	orange	741
▲	light brown	407
●	brown	420
✳	dark brown	839
⊠	light pink	776
Z	pink	335

OUTLINES

▢	blue	799
▢	bright green	907
▢	orange	741
▢	dark brown	839

Embroider this juicy apple on a blouse, or it will also look lovely on a tea towel.

Beat the heat

Embroider an attractive and useful potholder on easily worked, large-squared Aida fabric. One will be useful, or make a whole set and hang them in a row.

Size About 15 cm square; motif 4.5 x 7 cm

MATERIALS

20 cm square of white 8-count Aida fabric

15 cm square piece of matching cotton for the back

15 cm square piece of pre-washed flannel

80 cm red bias binding

DMC perle cotton No.5 in the colours of the required motif

Tapestry needle size 22

MOTIF FOR BLUE TEAPOT

DMC COLOUR KEY

●	red	321
=	yellow	742
○	green	704
▲	blue	825
✕	light blue	813

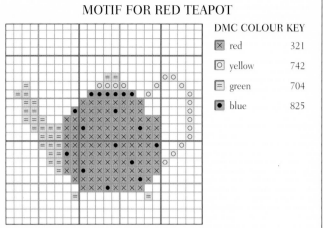

MOTIF FOR RED TEAPOT

DMC COLOUR KEY

☒	red	321
◻	yellow	742
⊟	green	704
●	blue	825

EMBROIDERY

Following the required graph, embroider the motif in cross stitch in the centre of the fabric. Use one thread of perle cotton, and work over one fabric square. Using blue, work a frame of one row of alternating crosses around the teapot: position this eleven squares from the top and bottom of the motif, seven squares from the left-hand side, and eight squares from the right-hand side. Cut the embroidery into a 15 cm square piece with the blue frame in the centre.

ASSEMBLY

Baste the embroidered front and back together with wrong sides facing and with the flannel inserted between, rounding the corners of all layers. Finish the edges with bias binding. For the hanger, sew the long sides of a 12 cm piece of bias binding double. Fold it double and sew it with a turning against the back of the left-hand corner.

Vary the colours of the teapot to match your kitchen scheme. Just make it really bright and cheerful.

A delightful and easy way to personalise a tablecloth—scatter cross-stitched pink rosebuds across it. Work as many or as few as you wish.

Scatter rosebuds

Size About 145 cm square

MATERIALS

1.50 m square piece of red and white checked hardanger fabric with about eight double fabric threads per 1 cm

DMC stranded embroidery cottons in the colours indicated on the colour key

Tapestry needle size 24

1 cm turned under, and making neat mitred corners.

NOTE

If this particular hardanger fabric is not available, other checked evenweave fabrics may be substituted, but the checks should be at least twenty-five Aida squares or fifty double fabric threads wide to fit the rose motif.

Red and white checks are an effective background for the rosebuds.

ROSEBUD MOTIF

DMC COLOUR KEY

⊡	light pink	3326
▼	pink	309
⊟	light green	369
☒	green	367

ROSA PROVINCIALIS AND FORGET-ME-NOT
Gouache painted for William III by Alexander Marshall, c. 1680
By gracious permission of H.M. The King

The motif is so quick to stitch and even a few will look lovely.

EMBROIDERY

Following the graph, embroider several rosebuds over the hardanger fabric. Work in cross stitch over two double fabric threads, using three strands of embroidery cotton. Position the motifs as preferred in and around the large square of the cloth. If desired, refer to the photograph for their position.

TO FINISH

Finish the tablecloth with a 2 cm wide hem with about

Sachets filled with fragrant lavender or pot pourri make delightful gifts, and they're so easy to make. Fashion them in any style, traditional, country or romantic, to suit your taste.

Fragrance of spring

Fragrant sachets add a touch of luxury — tuck this pink checked one into an underwear drawer or among a shelf of linens, or hang a lace-edged one among the clothes in a wardrobe.

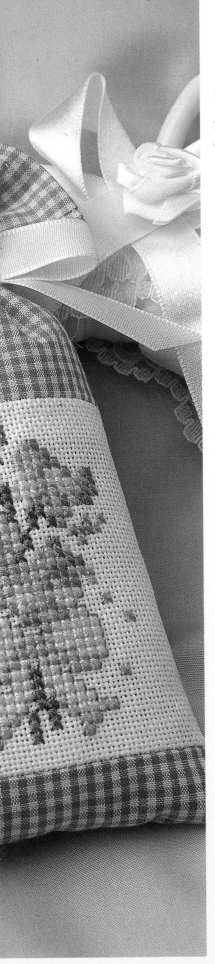

PINK AND WHITE CHECKED SACHET

Size Sachet 15 x 7 cm; motif about 6 x 4 cm

MATERIALS

10 cm square piece of white cotton evenweave fabric with eleven threads per 1 cm

30 x 10 cm piece of pink and white checked cotton fabric

DMC stranded embroidery cottons in the colours of the motif (flower bouquet with bow)

Tapestry needle size 24

30 cm of 1 cm wide very pale pink ribbon

Dried lavender or pot pourri

EMBROIDERY

Following the graph, embroider the motif in cross stitch in the centre of the evenweave fabric. Work each cross over two fabric threads, using two strands of embroidery cotton. When all cross stitching is complete, work the outlines in back stitch, using one strand of cotton: work the outlines of the blue flower in dark blue (799) and of the bow and pink flower in dark pink (603). Cut the embroidered piece to measure 8.5 cm high and 9 cm wide, with the motif in the centre.

TO ASSEMBLE

From pink and white checked cotton cut one 9 cm square piece and one 18.5 x 9 cm piece. With right sides facing and using 1 cm wide seams, sew the small piece to the top of the embroidery and the large piece to the bottom, forming a 32 cm long strip. Fold this piece double with right sides facing (about 1.5 cm of pink and white checked fabric should now be showing on the lower edge of the embroidery). Sew the sides with 1 cm seams. Turn the sachet right side out. Make a 5 mm double hem on the top edge. Fill about three-quarters full with lavender or pot pourri and close the sachet with ribbon tied into a bow.

FRAGRANT HANGING SACHET

Size Including lace 11.5 x 10 cm; motif 6 x 4 cm

MATERIALS

15 cm square piece of white 14-count Aida fabric

15 cm square piece of white cotton for the back

DMC stranded embroidery cottons in the colours of the blue-purple butterfly motif on page 68

Tapestry needle size 24

42 cm of 1.5 cm wide white pre-gathered lace

16 cm of 1 cm wide white ribbon

Dried lavender or pot pourri

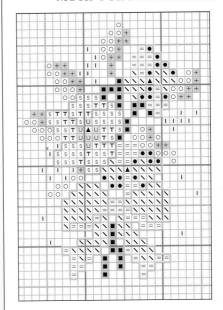

MOTIF FOR PINK CHECKED SACHET

DMC COLOUR KEY

○	light green	772
+	medium green	703
■	dark green	702
↘	light pink	818
=	medium pink	776
⊙	dark pink	603
s	light blue	3753
T	medium blue	3325
U	dark blue	799
▲	dark yellow	725
I	dark purple	210

OUTLINES

☐	dark pink	603
☐	dark blue	799

EMBROIDERY

Following the graph, embroider the motif in the centre of the Aida fabric. Work the embroidery in the same way as described for the pink and white checked sachet, working each cross over one Aida fabric square. Work the outlines of the butterfly in dark blue (792), of the flowers in very dark purple (553) and the leaves in dark green (702). When completed, cut the piece so that it measures 10.5 x 9 cm, with the motif in the centre.

TO ASSEMBLE

Sew the short ends of the lace together with a narrow french seam. Fold the ribbon double, and place it on the right side of the embroidery at centre top, with all raw edges aligned. Place the lace on the right side of the embroidery, just inside the seam allowance, with the decorative edge facing inwards. Baste in place, adjusting surplus width to give extra fullness

Centre: The pretty white Aida sachet is cross stitched in unusual colours.

at the corners. Sew in place. Centre the backing fabric over the embroidered piece/ribbon/lace with right sides facing, and trim to size. Sew all around, leaving an opening on one side for turning. Cut away the seam corners, turn cushion right side out. Fill three-quarters full with dried lavender or pot pourri. Slip stitch closed.

WHITE AIDA SACHET

Size Sachet 15 x 8 cm, motif 7.5 x 4 cm

MATERIALS

10 x 35 cm piece of white 14-count Aida fabric

DMC stranded embroidery cottons in the colours of the brown butterfly motif

Tapestry needle size 24

18 cm of 1.25 cm wide pre-gathered white lace

35 cm of 1 cm wide white ribbon

Dried lavender or pot pourri

EMBROIDERY

Fold the fabric in half, forming the front and back of the sachet. Finger-press the fold. Fold the piece open again. Following the graph, embroider the motif eight fabric squares above the fold, in the centre of the fabric (front of sachet). Work the embroidery in the same way

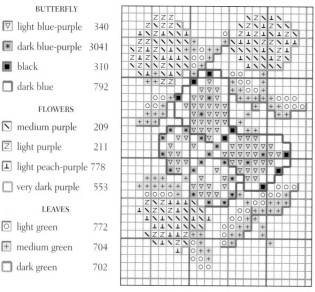

DMC COLOUR KEY		
BUTTERFLY		
▽ light blue-purple	340	
✳ dark blue-purple	3041	
■ black	310	
☐ dark blue	792	
FLOWERS		
↖ medium purple	209	
Z light purple	211	
⊥ light peach-purple	778	
☐ very dark purple	553	
LEAVES		
○ light green	772	
+ medium green	704	
☐ dark green	702	

MOTIF FOR HANGING SACHET

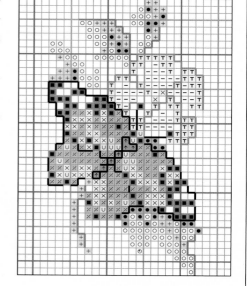

DMC COLOUR KEY	
○ light green	772
+ medium green	704
● dark green	702
T dark pink	601
− pink	604
✕ yellow	973
■ black	310
⊠ ochre	921
U grey-purple	3042
↑ dark red	902
OUTLINES	
☐ dark green	702
☐ black	310
☐ dark pink	601

MOTIF FOR WHITE AIDA SACHET

as for the pink and white checked sachet, but work each cross over one Aida fabric square. Work the outlines of the flower in dark pink (601), of the butterfly in black and of the leaves in dark green (702).

TO ASSEMBLE

Fold the fabric double with right sides facing, and sew the sides using 1 cm wide seams. Turn the sachet right side out. Make a 1 cm wide single turning on the top edge and baste. Join the short edges of the lace, using a narrow french seam. Sew the lace to the inside of the top edge, working small stitches. Fill the sachet three-quarters full with lavender or pot pourri and close the sachet with ribbon tied into a bow.

FRAGRANT CUSHION

Size Sachet 11 cm square; motif 5 x 4 cm

MATERIALS

10 cm square piece of white cotton evenweave fabric with eleven threads per 1 cm

Two 13 cm square pieces of blue flowered cotton fabric for the front and back (or one 13 cm square piece for the back, and two 9 x 4 cm and two 13 x 4 cm strips for the front: see method)

DMC stranded embroidery cottons in the colours of the blue-yellow pansy motif

Tapestry needle size 24

60 cm of 3 mm wide matching blue ribbon

Dried lavender or pot pourri

EMBROIDERY

Embroider the motif in the same way as described for the pink and white checked sachet.

Work the outlines using dark blue (799). When completed, cut the piece to measure 9 cm square, with the motif in the centre of the piece.

TO ASSEMBLE

With right sides uppermost, sew the embroidered piece in the centre of one piece of the blue

This fragrant cushion sachet has a real country feel.

flowered cotton. To do this, baste and press the raw edges of the embroidered piece under 1 cm, and using two strands of dark blue (799), sew it in place with running stitches, closely along the fold. Work the running stitches over three fabric threads and under two. (Or, assemble the front of the sachet by sewing 4 cm wide blue flowered strips around the embroidered piece, making 1 cm wide seams. Then add a blue frame of running stitches as described. Position this frame two fabric threads inside the seam of the embroidered piece.)

Using 1 cm wide seams, sew the front and back together with

right sides facing, leaving an opening on one side for turning. Cut away seam corners and turn the cushion right side out. Fill three-quarters full with dried lavender or pot pourri and slip stitch the opening closed. Make four small bows from the blue ribbon and sew or glue one to each corner of the embroidered piece.

MOTIF FOR CUSHION	DMC COLOUR KEY		
	○ light green	772
	+ medium green	703
	● dark pink	603
	S light blue	3753
	T medium blue	3325
	U dark blue	799
	▲ dark yellow	725
	- light yellow	727
	I dark purple	210
	□ light purple	211
	◆ black	310
	OUTLINES	
	□ dark blue	799

Sports special

Every cyclist needs a pouch and this one is lots of fun to wear.

Welcome ideas for any sports enthusiast— make an embroidered ball holder for a tennis player or a useful pouch for a cyclist. Both are made from evenweave fabric with clever cross-stitch motifs.

TENNIS BALL HOLDER

Size Length 26 cm

MATERIALS

26 x 35 cm piece of blue evenweave fabric with seven threads per 1 cm

DMC stranded embroidery cottons in the colours indicated on the colour key

Tapestry needle size 24

60 cm red bias binding

25 cm long yellow zipper

24 x 25 cm piece of red plastic

Strong cardboard

CUTTING OUT

From evenweavefabric cut one 26 cm square and two 8.5 cm diameter circles. From cardboard, cut two 7.5 cm diameter circles.

EMBROIDERY

Following the graph, embroider the motif in cross stitch over the evenweave fabric. Work each cross over two fabric threads, using four strands of embroidery cotton. Start the embroidery in the right-hand lower corner at 'A', 1 cm from the side edge, and 8 cm from top edge. Embroider the grid of the racquet in straight stitches, using light grey (762).

TO ASSEMBLE

Place the plastic underneath the embroidered piece. Fold a 1 cm seam at the top edge of the embroidered piece inwards, over the plastic, and sew the zipper in place below. Using 5 mm wide seams, sew the blue circles to the holder, with wrong sides together. Finish the seams with bias binding. Insert the cardboard circles inside the holder.

CYCLIST'S POUCH

Size 15 x 25 cm

MATERIALS

27 x 32 cm piece of red evenweave fabric with seven threads per 1 cm

DMC stranded embroidery cottons in the colours indicated on the colour key

Tapestry needle size 24

25 cm long blue zipper

3 cm wide elastic band

Buckle to close the elastic

EMBROIDERY

From red fabric cut a 19 x 27 cm piece and one 14.5 x 27 cm piece. Following the graph, embroider motif in the centre of small piece. Work in cross stitch over two fabric threads, using full six-stranded cottons. When all cross stitching is complete, work outlines in back stitch using three strands of black cotton.

TO ASSEMBLE

Fold under 1 cm at the top edge of both red pieces, and sew the zipper in place below. Cut the elastic into two equal pieces. Place the fabric pieces together with right sides facing, and sew the sides and lower edge, using 1 cm wide seams, at the same time joining the elastic at each side. Attach the buckle to the ends of the elastic band.

70

MOTIF FOR POUCH

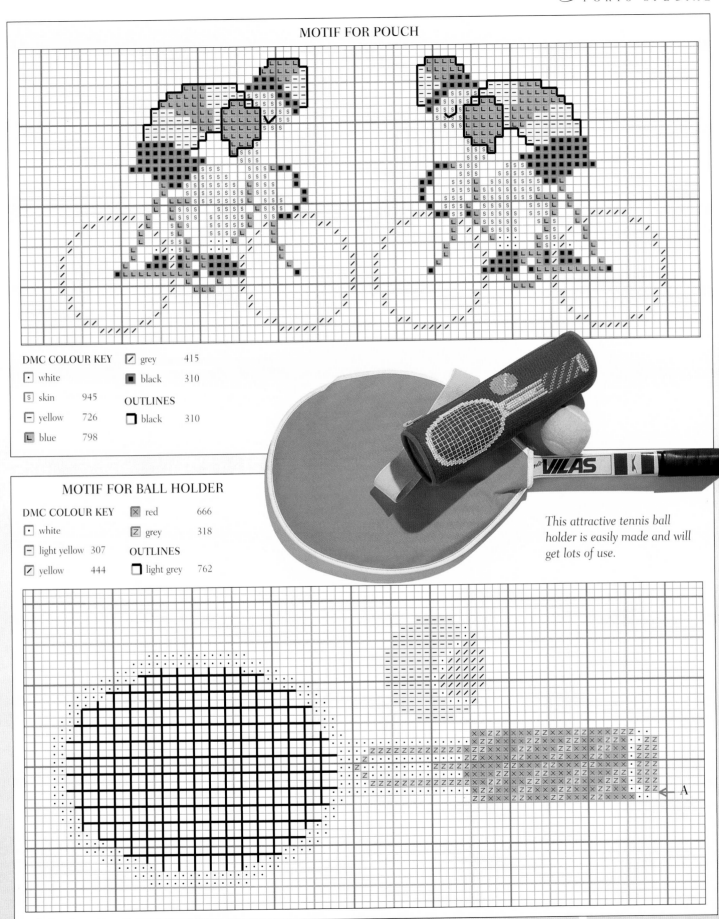

DMC COLOUR KEY

⊡ white		
s skin	945	
− yellow	726	
L blue	798	

☑ grey	415
■ black	310

OUTLINES

☐ black	310

MOTIF FOR BALL HOLDER

DMC COLOUR KEY

⊡ white	
− light yellow	307
☑ yellow	444

✗ red	666
Z grey	318

OUTLINES

☐ light grey	762

This attractive tennis ball holder is easily made and will get lots of use.

A

Embroider hardanger or Aida band with these charming motifs and add a fine touch to your home. Use the borders to edge shelves or sew them to sheets or towels.

Border beauty

Size 6 cm wide

MATERIALS

6 cm wide white hardanger band with nine double fabric threads per 1 cm, or white-edged 4.5 cm wide Aida band, as long as required plus 2 cm extra for seams

DMC stranded embroidery cottons in the colours indicated on the colour keys on pages 74

Tapestry needle size 24

EMBROIDERY

Following the graphs, embroider the selected motif in the centre of the band; follow the alphabet graph for the letters of the required name. If using hardanger, work in cross stitch over two double fabric threads using three strands of embroidery cotton; if using Aida band work over one square, using two strands of embroidery cotton. Work the motif of the house, and all narrow outer borders, over the entire length of the band.

TO FINISH

Turn the ends under 1 cm. Sew the embroidered band on a sheet or towel, or tack it to the front of a shelf.

ALPHABET FOR BORDERS

A line of washing, a row of houses, vases of flowers or your very own name—choose any of these unusual motifs for an embroidered band.

MOTIFS FOR BORDERS

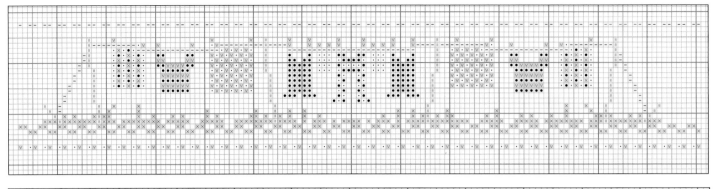

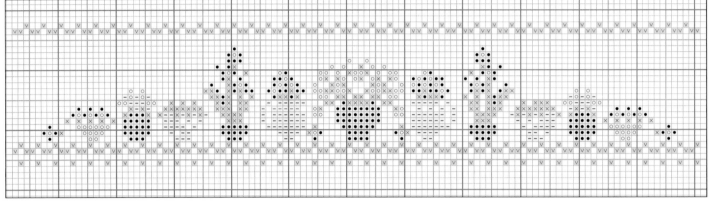

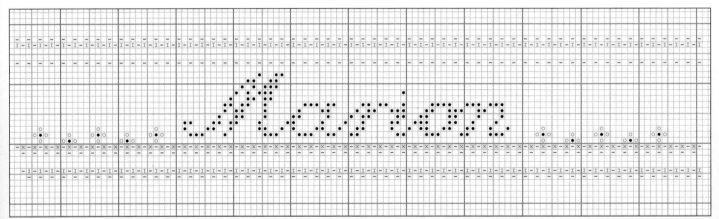

DMC COLOUR KEY

•	light yellow	727	/	turquoise	912
O	bright yellow	307	X	green	704
I	yellow	444	−	light blue	519
•	light pink	894	V	blue	996
Z	pink	603	II	brown	437

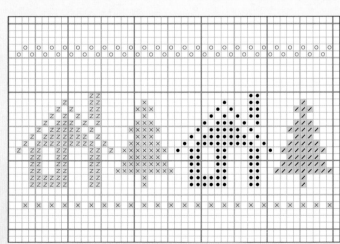

Pandora's box

Who could resist opening this delightful little box? Decorated with a cross-stitched waratah and some bright ribbons, it will add a personal touch to a small gift, at Christmas or any time.

A bright red waratah fits neatly on this small, oval box lid, but the idea can be adapted to suit any size or shape of box lid.

Size Motif about 6 x 2.5 cm

MATERIALS

7 x 9 cm oval box, wooden or papier mâché

15 cm square piece of cream 14-count Aida fabric

DMC stranded embroidery cottons in the colours indicated on the colour key

Tapestry needle size 24

30 cm of 1.5 cm wide green-red-gold checked ribbon

10 cm of 5 mm wide red ribbon

Craft glue

EMBROIDERY

Following the graph, embroider the waratah motif in the centre of the fabric. Work in cross stitch over one fabric square, using two strands of embroidery cotton in the indicated colour.

ASSEMBLY

Using pencil and paper, trace around the oval lid of the box. Add a 1 cm seam allowance all around and cut out the paper pattern. Place the pattern over the embroidered piece, ensuring that the waratah motif is in the centre, and cut out. Glue the embroidered piece on top of the lid so that the seams extend 1 cm beyond the top,

clip the curves of the seam and glue the seam to the sides of the lid. Glue checked ribbon around the sides of the lid, aligning the lower edges of both. Glue red ribbon over the sides of the lid (covering part of the Aida fabric and checked ribbon), aligning the top edges of both. Glue a length of red ribbon around the lower edge of the box.

WARATAH MOTIF FOR BOX

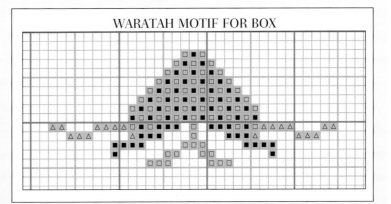

DMC COLOUR KEY

▢ bright red	666
■ dark red	498
△ green	905

Nice and cosy

Quickly made, this embroidered teacosy with colourful bias binding pops right over the teapot for maximum heat retention.

Size About 30 x 40 cm

MATERIALS

50 x 95 cm piece of white hardanger fabric with nine double fabric threads per 1 cm

75 x 100 cm white cotton fabric

DMC stranded embroidery cottons in pink (776), blue (519) and yellow (744)

Tapestry needle size 24

95 cm of pink and 95 cm of yellow bias binding, 1 cm wide

Polyester fibrefill or batting

Pattern paper

CUTTING OUT

From hardanger fabric cut two 40 x 45 cm pieces for the outer cosy and one 7 x 93 cm strip for the gusset. Enlarge the pattern graph for the teacosy, and cut out the paper pattern. With running stitches, outline the pattern shape on the two 40 x 45 cm pieces of hardanger, 6 cm from the lower edge.

EMBROIDERY

Following the graph, embroider the motifs within the marked outline of one piece. Work in cross stitch over two double fabric threads, using two strands of embroidery cotton. Use colours as preferred, and determine the position of the motifs with small pieces of paper. Refer to the photograph if desired. If motifs are required on both sides of cosy, repeat embroidery on other piece of hardanger.

MAKING OUTER COSY

When sewing, join all pieces with wrong sides together, using 5 mm seams.

So simple but nice: multi-coloured pastel stars are cross-stitched on one or both sides of this teacosy.

PATTERN FOR TEACOSY

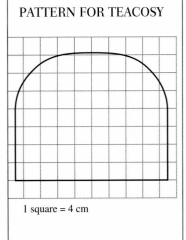

1 square = 4 cm

pieces, along the curved edge. Turn one cosy right side out, and slip this over the other cosy. Insert filling or batting between them. Sew the lower edges closed, with the seams turned inwards.

To finish

Put the inner cosy into the outer cosy. Fold the 6 cm wide hem of the outer cosy inwards and sew in place on the inner cosy with 1 cm turning.

STAR MOTIF

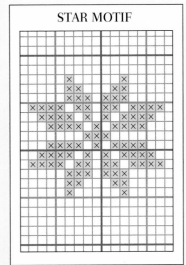

Cut the hardanger cosy shapes 5 mm outside the marked line, but 6 cm outside the line at the lower edge. Sew the 7 x 93 cm strip between the front and back pieces, along the curved edge. Finish one seam with pink bias binding, and the other seam with yellow bias binding.

Making inner cosy

The inner cosy consists of two cotton layers, with filling between them.

Cut the cosy shape four times from white cotton, adding 1 cm wide seam allowances, and cut two 8 x 73 cm strips for the gussets. Sew each gusset between two cosy

This lovely placemat can double as a tray-cloth for a luxury breakfast in bed. Work the outlines to suit your placement of the motif.

In your place

Make a special meal even more special with a set of these lovely placemats. They'll get lots of use, for birthdays, romantic anniversary dinners or holiday lunches. Substitute red for pink and you even have a festive Christmas mat.

Size About 39 x 26.5 cm; motif 7 x 5.5 cm

MATERIALS

45 x 32 cm piece of white 11-count Aida fabric

45 x 32 cm piece of white lining fabric

DMC stranded embroidery cottons in the colours indicated on the colour key

Tapestry needle size 24

EMBROIDERY

Following the graph for the border, work around the Aida fabric in cross stitch. Work each cross over one fabric square, using two strands of dark pink (899). Position the border about 3 cm inside the edges: the border should have twenty-four scallops (including the corner scallops) on the long side, and sixteen scallops (including the corner scallops) on the short sides.

Following the topiary graph, work the topiary motif in the left-hand top corner, four fabric squares from the border at the top (one long side), and nine fabric squares from the border at the right-hand side. Work in cross stitch over one fabric square, using three strands of cotton. When all cross stitching is complete, work the outlines in back stitch, using two strands of embroidery cotton.

TO FINISH

When the cross stitching is complete, sew the embroidered front and the back together with right sides facing, stitching two fabric squares outside the outermost stitches of the border, and leaving a small opening for turning on one side. Trim the seams, and cut away the seam corners. Turn the placemat right side out and handsew the opening closed.

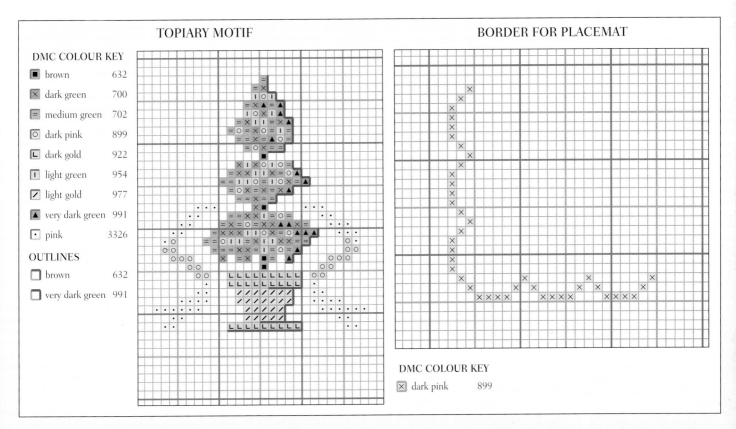

TOPIARY MOTIF

DMC COLOUR KEY

■	brown	632
☒	dark green	700
⊟	medium green	702
◎	dark pink	899
L	dark gold	922
I	light green	954
╱	light gold	977
▲	very dark green	991
·	pink	3326

OUTLINES

☐	brown	632
☐	very dark green	991

BORDER FOR PLACEMAT

DMC COLOUR KEY

☒	dark pink	899

A gift for baby

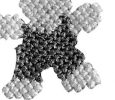

Little T-shirts and singlets for baby can quickly be given a personal touch with a cross-stitch motif. Use an initial, bear or rabbit, or choose one of the other motifs in the book.

A useful and economical gift for the new baby: a monogrammed T-shirt.

T-SHIRT WITH INITIAL

Size Letter about 2.5 cm high

MATERIALS

5 cm square piece of 10-count waste canvas (ten stitches to 2.5 cm)

Small quantity of DMC stranded embroidery cotton in required colour

Crewel needle size 7

White cotton t-shirt

Optional: different coloured buttons

METHOD

Baste the canvas on the right side of the T-shirt over the area to be embroidered: the photograph shows the position of the initial.

Following the alphabet graph, embroider the desired letter in cross stitch. Work each cross through both layers, over two fabric threads, using four strands of embroidery cotton. Keep the needle perpendicular to canvas while working, and stitch only through canvas holes, not the canvas threads. When completed, dampen canvas and remove basting and canvas threads one by one with tweezers. Replace white buttons of the T-shirt with brightly coloured ones.

SINGLET WITH RABBIT

Size Motif about 3 cm square

MATERIALS

White baby singlet

Small piece of 14-count waste canvas (fourteen stitches to 2.5 cm)

DMC stranded embroidery cotton in blue (799)

Crewel needle size 8

METHOD

Baste the waste canvas on the front of the singlet over the area to be embroidered. Following the graph, embroider the motif in cross stitch. Work each cross through both layers over two canvas threads, using two strands of embroidery cotton. Keep the needle perpendicular to the canvas while you

So quick and easy to stitch, this blue bunny has a certain style.

work and stitch only through the canvas holes, not the canvas threads. When complete, dampen the canvas and remove the basting and canvas threads one by one with tweezers.

If preferred, crochet a border around the edges of the singlet or use a row of blanket stitches in blue.

SINGLET WITH BEAR

Size Motif 4 x 4.5 cm

MATERIALS

White baby singlet

DMC stranded embroidery cottons in the colours indicated on the colour key

Crewel needle size 8

Small piece of 14-count waste canvas (fourteen stitches to 2.5 cm)

METHOD

Baste the waste canvas on the front of the singlet over the area to be embroidered: if necessary, refer to the photograph for its position. Following the

ALPHABET FOR T-SHIRT

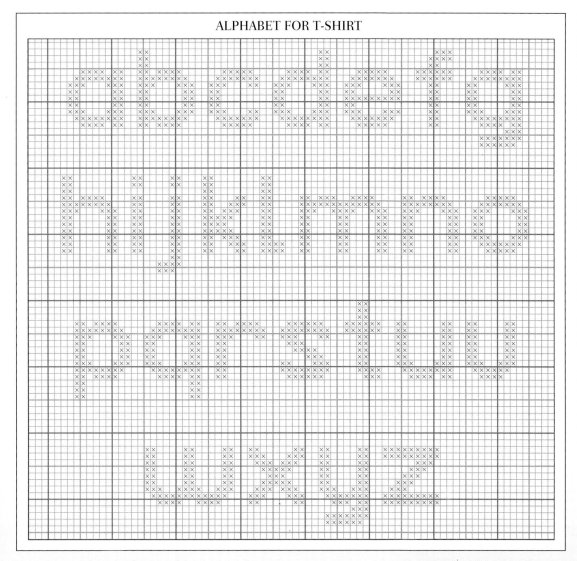

MOTIF FOR BUNNY

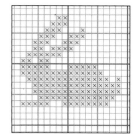

Add a cute little bear to a singlet for instant appeal.

graph, embroider the bear motif in cross stitch. Work each cross through both layers over two canvas threads, using two strands of embroidery cotton. Keep the needle perpendicular to the canvas while working, and stitch only through the canvas holes, not the canvas threads. When the cross stitching is complete, work the outlines in back stitch, using ochre (977), and work the eyes in french knots using dark grey (413).

When stitching is complete, dampen the canvas and remove the basting and canvas threads one by one with tweezers.

MOTIF FOR BEAR

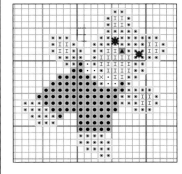

DMC COLOUR KEY

✻ light yellow 3078		▲ dark grey	413
I yellow	726	☒ pink	776
⊡ light pink	818	**OUTLINES**	
● dark blue	798	☐ dark grey	413
		☐ ochre	977

This sweet sampler and ring cushion with evocative motifs will provide a lasting memento of the wedding.

A wedding will be long remembered with these beautiful cross-stitched souvenirs decorated with bluebirds, hearts, rings, crowns and flowers.

Wedding bells

WEDDING SAMPLER

Size Outer edge of frame 16 x 19.5 cm, frame width 1.5 cm; embroidery 9 x 12 cm

MATERIALS

20 x 25 cm piece of white 14-count Aida fabric

DMC stranded embroidery cottons in the colours indicated on the colour keys on pages 83 and 84

Tapestry needle size 24

White picture frame

EMBROIDERY

Following the graph for the sampler, embroider the motifs in the centre of the fabric in cross stitch. Work the required names from the alphabet graph, using pink-brown (452), positioning the top name two squares below the heart and the bottom name three squares below the rings. Work in cross stitch over one fabric square, using two strands of embroidery cotton. Work the straight line of the border in back stitch, using two strands of pink-brown (452), positioning it one fabric square outside the bird motifs at the sides, and two squares outside the motifs at the top and bottom. Complete the border from the graph.

TO FINISH

Frame the completed embroidery, leaving about twelve squares of fabric outside the border.

WEDDING RING CUSHION

Size Cushion 16 x 10.5 cm without lace

MATERIALS

20 x 15 cm piece of white 14-count Aida fabric

DMC stranded embroidery cottons in gold (729), dark blue (799), light blue (800) and pink-brown (452)

Tapestry needle size 24

20 x 15 cm piece of matching fabric for the back

50 cm of 4 mm wide craft pearl trimming

65 cm of 4.5 cm wide pre-gathered white lace

Polyester fibrefill

EMBROIDERY

Following the graph for the sampler, embroider the rings, the bluebirds and crown in the centre of the Aida fabric (one long side forms the lower side). Work in cross stitch over one fabric square, using two strands of embroidery cotton. Work the rings in the centre of the fabric in gold. Position the crown four fabric squares above the rings, working in dark blue (799). Embroider a bird motif on each side of the rings, one fabric square away, using light blue, with dark blue for the eye and gold for the beak. Position the motifs in such a way that the top edge of the birds will come two fabric squares higher than the rings. Work the names and date from the alphabet and number graphs, using pink-brown (452). Position the names three fabric squares from the top edge of the birds, and the date three fabric squares below the birds. When

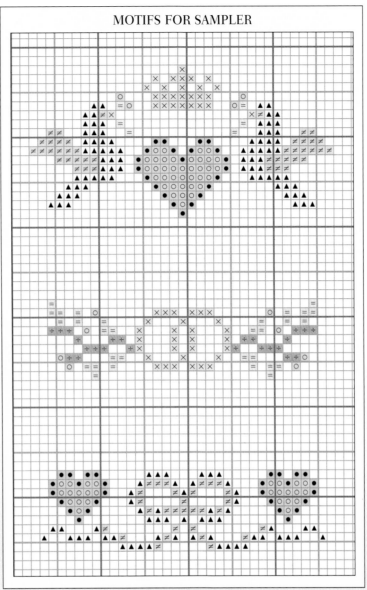

MOTIFS FOR SAMPLER

DMC COLOUR KEY

⊠	gold	729
▲	light blue	800
⋕	dark blue	799
◎	light pink	893
●	dark pink	892
=	light green	368
✛	dark green	988

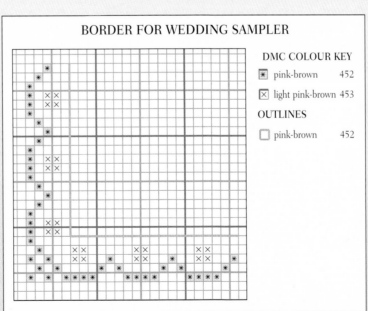

BORDER FOR WEDDING SAMPLER

DMC COLOUR KEY

✳	pink-brown	452
⊠	light pink-brown	453

OUTLINES

☐	pink-brown	452

The flower girl or pageboy will be so proud to carry this lovely ring cushion (the rings are safely tied on!).

the embroidery is completed, cut the fabric into an 18 x 12.5 cm rectangle, with the embroidery in the centre.

To assemble

Cut the backing the same size as the front. Using 1 cm wide seams, sew the two pieces together with the right sides

facing, leaving a small opening on one side for turning and filling. Cut away seam corners diagonally, and turn right side out. Fill lightly with fibrefill and sew the opening closed.

Join the two short ends of the lace with a narrow french seam. Sew the lace around the outer edge of the cushion,

against the back, arranging extra fullness at the corners. Sew the pearl trimming around the outer edge of the Aida fabric, on the front.

Cut the ribbon in half. Sew the pieces in the centre of the cushion, each about 2 cm outside the bluebirds, ready to tie on the wedding rings.

ALPHABET GRAPH FOR SAMPLER AND CUSHION

DMC COLOUR KEY

☒	pink-brown	452

ROSE SACHET

MOTIF FOR ROSE SACHET

DMC COLOUR KEY

s	light green	368	▣ light pink	3708
◎	medium pink	893	✕ dark green	988

Size About 11 x 5 cm

A miniature scented sachet is ideal to pop into the honeymoon suitcase or pack away with the wedding dress or veil.

MATERIALS

For one bag

30 cm of 5 cm wide self-edged white Aida band with six squares per 1 cm

DMC stranded embroidery cottons in the colours indicated on the colour key

Tapestry needle size 24

25 cm of 3 mm wide ribbon

Dried lavender

EMBROIDERY

Fold the band in half, and fingerpress the fold. Open band out again. Following the graph, embroider the selected motif in the centre of band, about seven fabric squares above fold (front of bag). Work in cross stitch over one fabric square, using two strands of embroidery cotton. Press completed embroidery from the back under a damp cloth.

TO FINISH

Turn the short ends of the embroidered band about 4 cm inwards, and fold the piece double with wrong sides facing. Using white sewing thread, sew the side edges closely inside the self-edged border. Fill the bag three-quarters full with lavender. Knot ribbon around the bag, about 3 cm from the top edge, and tie into a bow.

This cute checked cap with cross-stitched engine is sure to be a hit with the young.

Protect your little one from the sun with a trendy cap or sunhat with train motif. The sewing patterns are included.

Toot, toot!

CAP

Size To fit head circumference about 48 cm

MATERIALS

About 30 x 30 cm piece of blue-white checked cotton

About 30 x 50 cm piece of white cotton

Small quantities of DMC stranded embroidery cottons in the colours indicated on the colour key

Crewel needle size 8

Small piece of light yellow cotton

One self-cover button

Iron-on interfacing

8 cm square piece of 10-count waste canvas (ten stitches to 2.5 cm)

CUTTING OUT

Copy the pattern pieces on page 88. Adding 1 cm wide seam allowances, cut the crown piece six times each from the checked and white cotton fabrics, and the peak twice from white cotton.

EMBROIDERY

Baste the waste canvas over one checked piece: position it 1 cm from the lower edge. Following the graph, embroider the motif in cross stitch. Position it in the centre and 1.25 cm from the lower edge of the waste canvas. Work each cross, through both layers, over two canvas threads, using two strands of embroidery cotton. Keep needle perpendicular to the canvas while working, and stitch only through the canvas holes, not the canvas threads. When completed, dampen the canvas, and remove the basting and canvas threads one by one with tweezers.

TO ASSEMBLE

With right sides facing and using 1 cm seams, sew three crown pieces together, then sew the other three pieces together, and finally join the two triple pieces to complete the crown. Topstitch all seams. Work the white crown pieces the same way. Reinforce one peak with iron-on interfacing. Place the two peaks together with right sides facing, and sew the outside edge. Turn right side out. Topstitch the outside edge twice. Sew the peak to the checked crown piece.

Sew the white and checked crowns together with right sides facing along the lower edge, leaving a small opening in the seam for turning. Turn the cap right side out and sew the opening closed. Topstitch the crown closely along the lower edge. Cover the button with yellow cotton. Sew the button securely to the top through both layers.

SUNHAT

Size To fit head circumference about 48 cm

MATERIALS

60 x 60 cm piece of white cotton fabric

15 x 15 cm piece of white hardanger with nine double fabric threads per 1 cm

Small piece of pink cotton fabric

Iron-on interfacing

Small quantities of DMC stranded embroidery cottons in the colours indicated on the colour key

Tapestry needle size 24

1.40 m of narrow yellow bias binding

One self-cover button

CUTTING OUT

Copy the pattern pieces on page 88. Adding 1 cm wide seam allowance, cut the crown piece eleven times from white cotton and the brim twice on the fabric fold from white cotton. With running stitches, mark the outline of the crown piece on the white hardanger fabric.

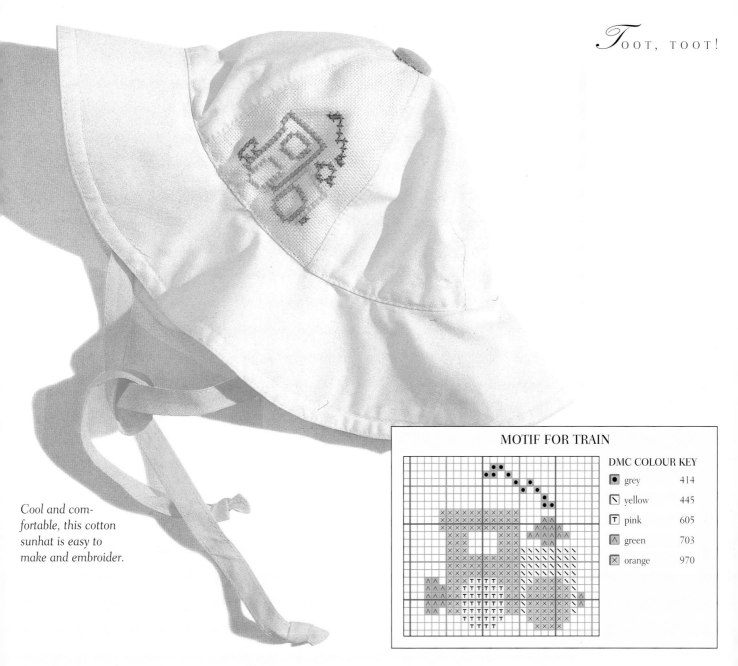

MOTIF FOR TRAIN

DMC COLOUR KEY

●	grey	414
◥	yellow	445
T	pink	605
∧	green	703
⊠	orange	970

Cool and comfortable, this cotton sunhat is easy to make and embroider.

EMBROIDERY

Following the graph, embroider the motif in the centre of marked hardanger piece, 1 cm from lower edge (= the marked line). Embroider only the outlines of various train sections. Work in cross stitch over two double fabric threads, using two strands of embroidery cotton. When completed, cut the crown piece 1 cm outside marked lines.

TO ASSEMBLE

With right sides facing and using 1 cm seams, sew three crown pieces together. Repeat four times. Sew two triple pieces together. Repeat. Topstitch all crown seams. Cut the bias binding into four pieces the same length. Sew two pieces together closely along the edge to form one tie. Repeat with the other two pieces.

Reinforce one brim with iron-on interfacing. Place the two brims together with right sides facing, and sew the outside edge. Trim the seams, and turn the brim right side out. Topstitch the brim twice along the outside edge. Sew the (double) brim to the crown with the embroidered piece. Topstitch the crown closely along the joining seam, at the same time joining the ties, opposite each other, on the inside of the hat. Ensure that the train will be on the front of the hat. Place the inner crown inside the hat and sew the outer edge into place with a turning.

TO FINISH

Cover the button with pink cotton. Sew the button securely to the top of the crown through both layers. Make a knot in each tie end.

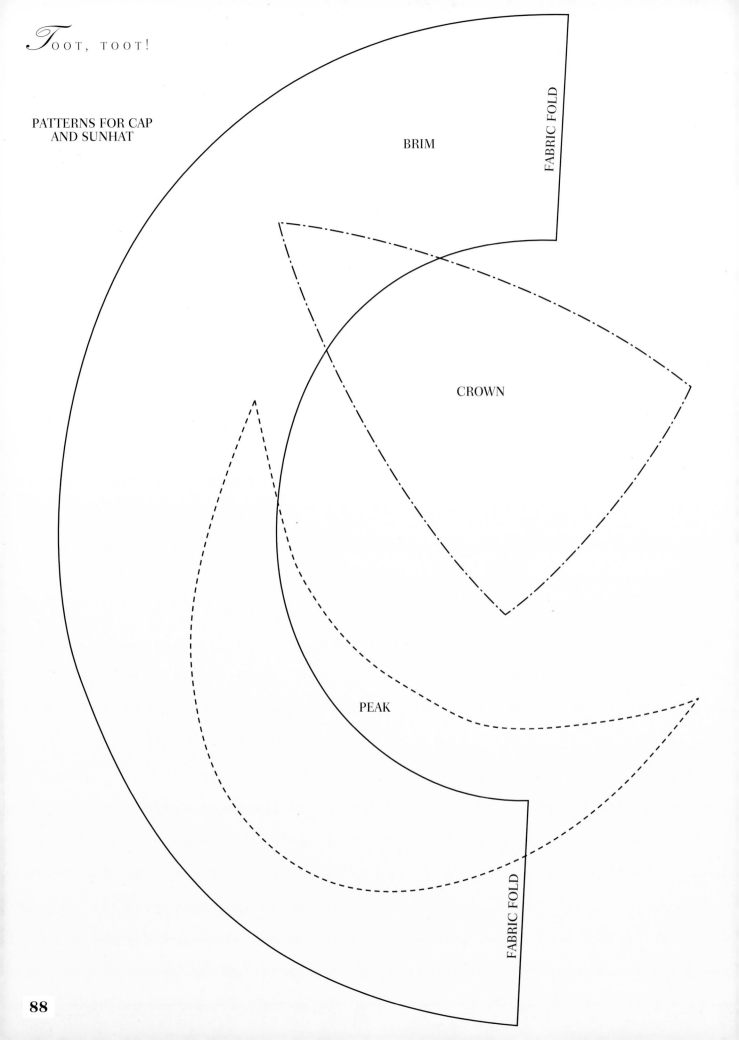

Toot, Toot!

PATTERNS FOR CAP
AND SUNHAT

BRIM

FABRIC FOLD

CROWN

PEAK

FABRIC FOLD

Decorate a cottonbud holder with these fine little horses— they're raring to go.

Pony tale

Size Band 7 cm high

MATERIALS

Clear plastic cotton bud holder

10 cm wide piece of white 11-count Aida fabric, as long as the circumference of the holder plus 2.5 cm

DMC stranded embroidery cottons in the colours indicated on the colour key

Tapestry needle size 24

MOTIF FOR HORSE

DMC COLOUR KEY

⊡	blue	792
▨	orange	721
⊠	yellow	973
▲	white	
■	black	310
▧	red	321

OUTLINES

▭	red	321

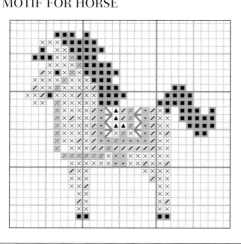

EMBROIDERY

Following the graph, embroider three horses in the centre of fabric, evenly spaced. Work in cross stitch over one Aida square, using three strands of embroidery cotton. Work the saddle details in straight stitch, using three strands of red cotton.

TO FINISH

Sew short sides together with a 1 cm seam, forming a continuous piece. Fold the top and bottom edges 1 cm inwards. Using four strands of embroidery cotton, work blanket stitches along edges: work each stitch two fabric squares deep and one square apart. When completed, cut off surplus seams closely next to the embroidery. Fit on holder.

Stitch a row of these jolly little horses with their colourful saddlecloths and you can brighten up any cylindrical container.

Christmas cheer

Bright cross-stitched patterns on a felt base make interesting new tree ornaments.

These small cross-stitched motifs can be embroidered in a few hours, and they'll give an unusual and delightful touch to your Christmas festivities.

TREE DECORATIONS

Size 6 cm diameter

MATERIALS

For one decoration

Two 8 cm square pieces of felt in different colours

DMC stranded embroidery cottons in the colours indicated on the colour key

8 cm square piece of linen with eight threads per 1 cm

Small amount polyester fibrefill

Red ribbon

Gold thread or cord

METHOD

Baste the linen on top of one piece of felt. Following the graph, embroider the motif in cross stitch. Work over two linen threads, through both layers, using four strands of embroidery cotton. Keep the needle perpendicular to the linen while working, and stitch only through the holes of the linen, not the threads. When completed, remove the linen threads one by one with tweezers.

TO FINISH

Place the two pieces of felt together with wrong sides facing and a small amount of filling between them. Sew together closely along the edge of the embroidery, using two strands of embroidery cotton. Cut off surplus felt close to the stitches.

Tie ribbon into a bow and attach it to the point of the ornament. Also attach golden thread or cord to the point for hanging the ornament.

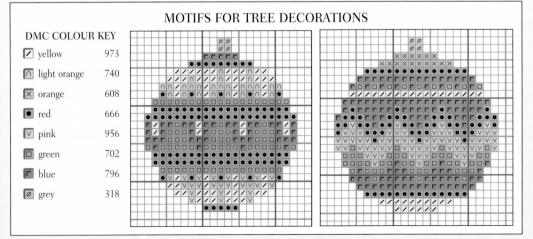

MOTIFS FOR TREE DECORATIONS

DMC COLOUR KEY

✓	yellow	973
∩	light orange	740
✕	orange	608
●	red	666
∨	pink	956
☐	green	702
⌐	blue	796
∅	grey	318

DECORATED POCKET

Size Motif 5.5 x 6 cm

MATERIALS

DMC stranded embroidery cottons in the colours indicated on the colour key

Crewel needle size 7

For each motif, a 10 cm square piece of 10-count waste canvas (ten stitches to 2.5 cm)

Red pyjamas with pocket (or make a pocket—finished size 10 x 9.5 cm—from matching fabric)

METHOD

Carefully unpick the pocket from the pyjamas. Baste the waste canvas on the right side of the pocket over the area to be embroidered: the lower edge of the bell should come about 1 cm from the lower edge of the finished pocket.

Following the graph, embroider the bell through both layers in cross stitch. Work each cross over two fabric threads, using three strands of the embroidery cotton. Keep the needle perpendicular to the canvas while working, and stitch only through the canvas holes, not the canvas threads. When all cross stitching is complete, work the outlines in back stitch, using two strands of cotton, in green around the bow, and yellow for the clapper.

Dampen the canvas, and remove the basting and canvas threads one by one with tweezers. Sew on pocket.

Turn purchased red pyjamas into special Christmas pyjamas with cross-stitched golden bells on the pockets. Waiting for Santa will be extra fun!

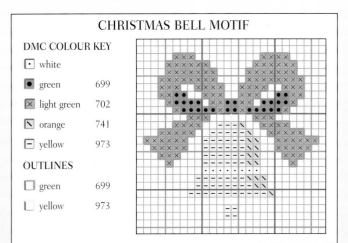

CHRISTMAS BELL MOTIF

DMC COLOUR KEY

⊡	white	
●	green	699
⊠	light green	702
⧅	orange	741
⊟	yellow	973

OUTLINES

☐	green	699
∟	yellow	973

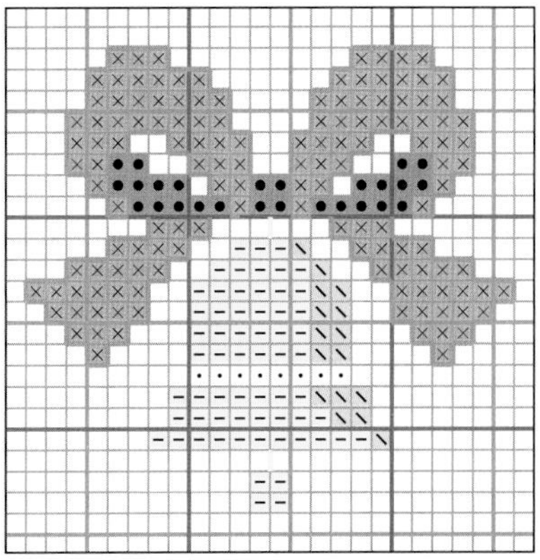

Add a touch of class to your Christmas table with cross-stitched napkins and rings.

CHRISTMAS NAPKIN AND RING

Size Napkin 28 cm square, motif 4 x 4.5 cm; ring 5 x 7 cm, motif 3 cm square

MATERIALS

30 cm square piece of white 14-count Aida fabric (for napkin)

20 cm of 5 cm wide gold-edged white Aida band, with six fabric squares per 1 cm for ring

DMC stranded embroidery cottons in the colours indicated on the colour key

Tapestry needle size 24

NAPKIN

Make a narrow double hem around the fabric. Following the graph, embroider the bauble motif in one corner, about 3.5 cm from the edges. When all cross stitching is complete, work the outlines in back stitch, using one strand of cotton: use gold (783) for the bauble and black (310) for the bow.

RING

Following the graph, embroider the star motif in the centre of the Aida band. When

STAR MOTIF FOR RING

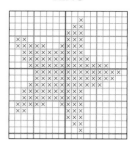

DMC COLOUR KEY

☒ dark yellow 725

BAUBLE MOTIF FOR NAPKIN

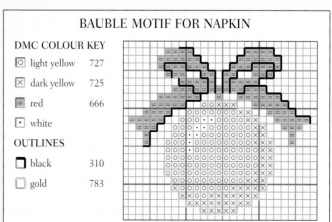

DMC COLOUR KEY

◎	light yellow	727
☒	dark yellow	725
☰	red	666
·	white	

OUTLINES

◻	black	310
◻	gold	783

Add to the traditional feel of your Christmas with cross-stitched place cards or tags.

This jolly Santa with gift makes a fun Christmas card for a special friend.

completed, cut the band to measure 16 cm, with the motif in the centre. Sew the short ends together with a narrow french seam, forming a ring.

CARD WITH SANTA

Size Card 13 x 9 cm; motif 4.5 x 3 cm

MATERIALS

Purchased 13 x 9 cm white card, with an 8.5 x 6.5 cm oval window

12 x 8.5 cm piece of white 14-count Aida fabric

DMC stranded embroidery cottons in the colours indicated on the colour key

Tapestry needle size 24

MOTIFS FOR TAGS OR PLACE CARDS

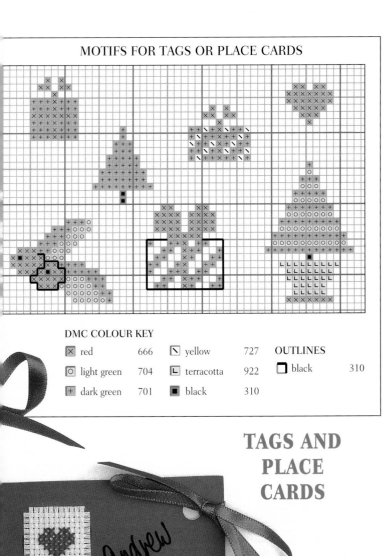

DMC COLOUR KEY

					OUTLINES	
☒ red	666	◩ yellow	727		☐ black	310
⊙ light green	704	L terracotta	922			
⊞ dark green	701	■ black	310			

TAGS AND PLACE CARDS

EMBROIDERY

Following the graph, embroider the desired motifs on the Aida fabric, leaving a distance of about 3 cm between each motif. Work in cross stitch over one fabric square, using two strands of embroidery cotton. Work any outlines in black, using one strand of cotton. When completed, cut out each embroidery two or three fabric squares outside the motif. Remove the threads of the outermost fabric square around each piece, forming a narrow fringe.

METHOD

Cut a 4 x 8 cm piece of cardboard for each tag/card. Glue the embroidered piece in the centre of the card, about 7.5 mm from the left-hand or bottom edge (one short side). For the place card, write the name on the right-hand side. For the tag, punch a hole in the right-hand top corner, and thread a piece of ribbon through the hole; tie in a bow.

SANTA MOTIF

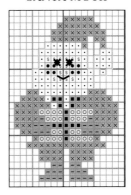

DMC COLOUR KEY

☒ red	321
⊙ yellow	742
⊟ blue	825
⊡ skin	951
■ green	701
⊡ white	
● pink	603

OUTLINES

☐ black	310
☐ gold	783

METHOD

Following the graph, embroider the motif in the centre of the fabric. Work in cross stitch over one fabric square, using two strands of embroidery cotton. When all cross stitching is complete, work the outlines in back stitch, using one strand of gold (783). Work the eyes with a french knot, and the mouth with a small V-stitch, using two strands of black. Press the completed embroidery from the back under a damp cloth, and glue it behind the window of the card.

Size About 4 x 8 cm

MATERIALS

For six tags or cards

Bright red and green cardboard

10 x 30 cm piece of white 14-count Aida fabric

Small quantities of DMC stranded embroidery cottons in the colours indicated on the colour key

Tapestry needle size 24

1.5 m of 5 mm wide ribbon in red or green

Craft glue

Hole puncher for the tags

Star signs

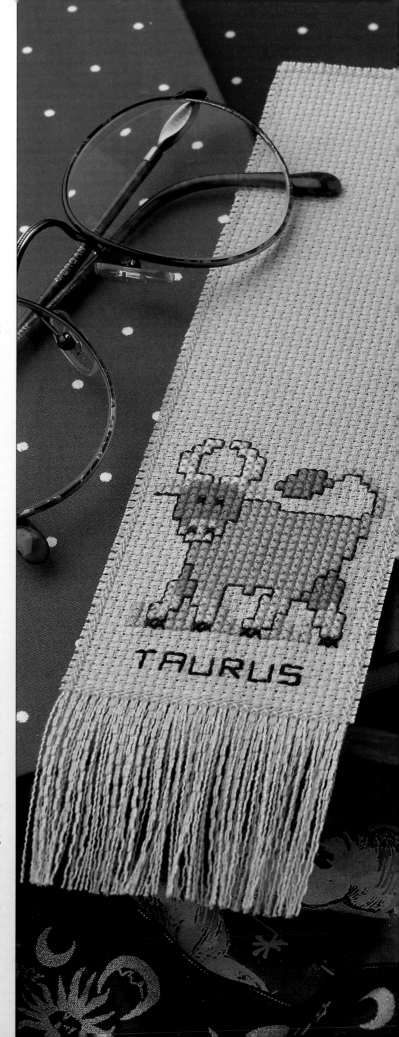

These beautiful zodiac signs make book-marks of distinction. Embroider one with your sign or delight your friends with their own zodiac bookmark.

Size Including fringe, about 20 x 6.5 cm

MATERIALS

For one bookmark

25 x 10 cm of 14-count Aida fabric in desired colour

Matching coloured sewing thread

DMC stranded embroidery cottons in the colours of the required motif

Tapestry needle size 24

About 17 x 6 cm iron-on mending patch in a colour to match the Aida fabric, or use white iron-on interfacing

EMBROIDERY

Following the graph, embroider the required motif in the centre of the Aida fabric, about 7.5 cm from the lower edge (one short side). Work in cross stitch over one fabric square, using two strands of embroidery cotton. When all cross stitching is complete, work the outlines in back stitch, using one strand of cotton.

Following the alphabet graph, work the zodiac name below the motif, using two strands of black cotton. If the required name is too long to fit the width of the bookmark,

Everyone knows their star sign and they'll enjoy using a zodiac bookmark with cross-stitched design and neat herringbone edging.

work the name lengthways above the motif, with the letters one below the other on the left-hand side or in the centre of the bookmark.

TO ASSEMBLE

On the embroidered piece, outline the shape of the bookmark with a row of closed herringbone stitches, using matching sewing thread. To do this, work each stitch over one fabric square, and position the bottom row three fabric squares below the zodiac name, the side rows one fabric square from the sides of the motif, and the top row about 11 cm above the motif. When completed, cut the sides and top edge closely along the herringbone stitching, taking care not to cut into the stitches.

Cut the lower edge about 4 cm from the stitching, and withdraw the horizontal fabric threads to form a 4 cm long fringe. Cut the mending patch or interfacing the same size as the bookmark (less the fringe), and iron it accurately against the back of the bookmark.

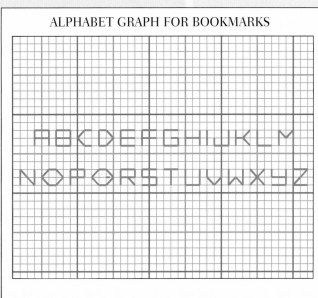

ALPHABET GRAPH FOR BOOKMARKS

STAR SIGN MOTIFS

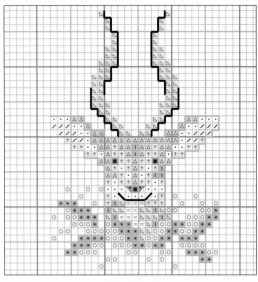

CAPRICORN

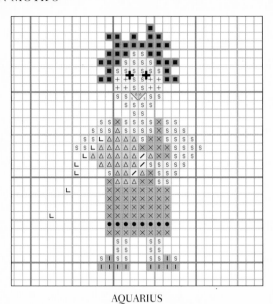

AQUARIUS

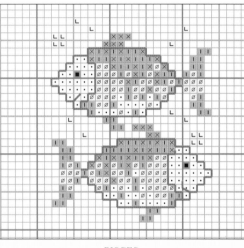

PISCES

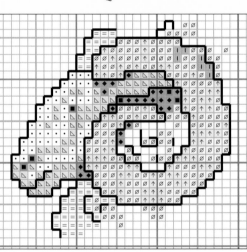

ARIES

TAURUS

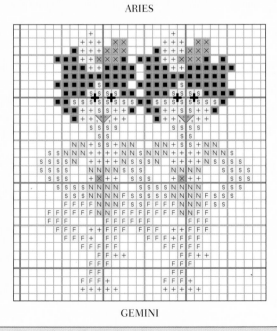

GEMINI

DMC COLOUR KEY

X	red	666
O	light green	472
✳	dark green	702
◹	light grey-blue	809
◆	dark grey-blue	413
●	dark blue	798
L	light blue	800
N	dark baby-blue	813
F	light baby-blue	827
+	pink	605
S	light skin	945
∅	light yellow	727
U	yellow	726
=	cream	822
·	white	
■	black	310
⊠	gold	676
↑	very light copper	353
╱	light copper	402
△	medium copper	922
I	dark copper	920
▲	very dark copper	919

OUTLINES

▢	red	666
▢	yellow	726
◼	black	310
▢	medium copper	922
◗	very dark copper	919

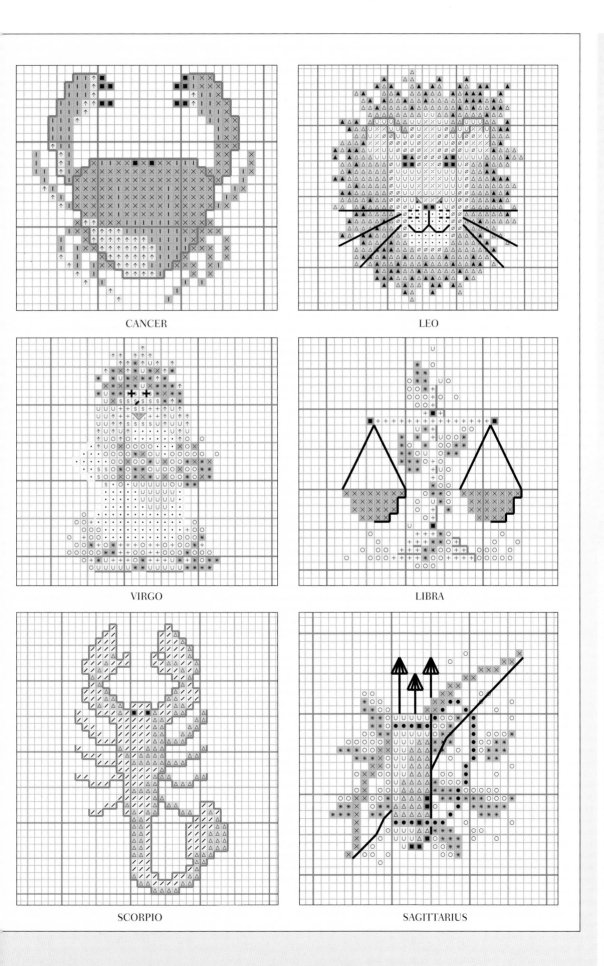

CANCER

LEO

VIRGO

LIBRA

SCORPIO

SAGITTARIUS

Congratulations!

Graduation day will be made extra special with this cheerful celebration card.

Birthdays, graduations, engagements, weddings, anniversaries— any special event will be made more memorable with a unique, handmade card that shows how much you care.

MARTINI

Size 16 cm square

MATERIALS

20 cm square piece of white hardanger fabric with nine double fabric threads per 1 cm

DMC stranded embroidery cottons in the colours indicated on the colour key

Tapestry needle size 24

16 x 32 cm piece of strong pink cardboard

15 cm square piece of thin white paper

Confetti

Craft knife

Craft glue

EMBROIDERY

Following the graph, embroider the motif in the centre of the hardanger. Work in cross stitch over two double fabric threads, using two strands of embroidery cotton. Work the outlines in back stitch, using two strands of black cotton. When completed, cut the embroidered piece to measure 14 cm square, with the motif in the centre.

TO FINISH

Score across the centre of the pink cardboard, on the right side, and fold the card double. Cut an 11 cm square window in the front of the card, 2.5 cm from the sides and lower edge. Glue the embroidery against the back of the window, and glue a sheet of white paper to the inside of the card to cover the back of the embroidery. Glue confetti to the front 'frame' of the card.

HEARTS GALORE

Size Card 10.5 x 15 cm

MATERIALS

For one card

Double card, with or without window

10 cm square piece of white 18-count Aida fabric (for the two rectangular motifs) or linen with eleven threads per 1 cm

Small quantities DMC stranded embroidery cottons in the colours on the colour key

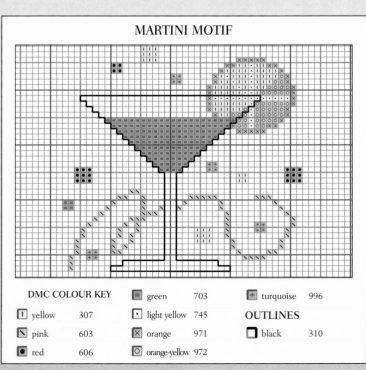

DMC COLOUR KEY		
▣ yellow 307	▣ green 703	⊞ turquoise 996
◩ pink 603	▪ light yellow 745	**OUTLINES**
● red 606	⊠ orange 971	☐ black 310
	◉ orange-yellow 972	

Tapestry needle size 26

Craft knife

Craft glue

10 x 14 cm piece of thin
white paper

EMBROIDERY

Following the graph, embroider
the desired motif in cross stitch
in the centre of the fabric. Use
Aida fabric for the two rectangular motifs, and linen for the
other two motifs. Work each
cross over one Aida square or
two threads of linen, using two
strands of embroidery cotton.
When all cross stitching is complete, work the outlines in back
stitch, using one strand of black
embroidery cotton.

TO ASSEMBLE

Fringe the fabric edges and
glue the embroidery onto the
front of the card. Or, if preferred, glue the embroidery
behind a window. For this, cut
out a rectangular, square or
heart-shaped window on the
front of the card. The pattern

for the heart-shaped window is
given on page 102. Copy onto
strong cardboard, and cut out.
Trace around the shape on the

front of the card, and cut out.
Glue white paper to the inside
of the card so that it covers the
back of the embroidery.

*For weddings,
engagements or
Valentine's Day—
cards with hearts will
suit many occasions.*

GRAPHS FOR HEARTS

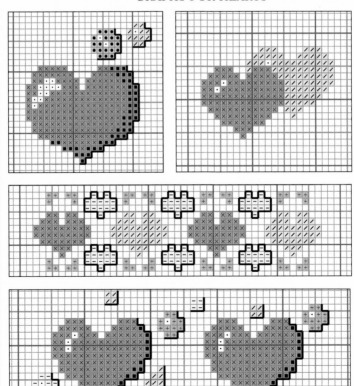

DMC COLOUR KEY

☐	white	
☒	red	666
■	dark red	321
☑	pink	604
⊟	yellow	726
⊞	turquoise	996
⊡	light blue	813

OUTLINES

☐	black	310

This lovely card is perfect for conveying birthday or anniversary congratulations. It could also be used as a get well card.

PATTERN FOR HEART-SHAPED WINDOW

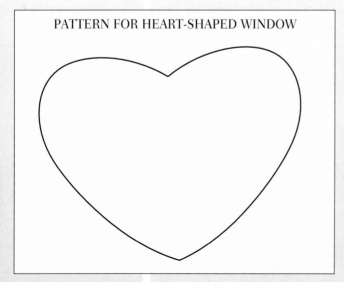

BASKET AND BOW

Size Card 15 x 11 cm; motif 7 x 5.5 cm

MATERIALS

Pale pink 15 x 11 cm purchased card, with an 11.5 x 8.5 cm oval window in centre front

15 x 12 cm piece of white 18-count Aida fabric

DMC stranded embroidery cottons in the colours indicated on the colour key

Tapestry needle size 26

EMBROIDERY

Following the graph, embroider the motif in cross stitch in the centre of the fabric. Work each cross over one fabric square, using two strands of embroidery cotton. When the stitching is completed, cut the embroidery to measure 13.5 x 10.5 cm, with the motif in the centre. Place the embroidery face down, cover it with a damp cloth and iron it. Glue the embroidered piece behind the window of the card.

BASKET AND BOW

DMC COLOUR KEY

⁒	light red	816	⊥	dark gold	780
✕	dark red	814	‖	light green	955
○	light pink	604	N	dark green	562
▽	dark pink	3687	·	light blue	800
⟍	light gold	783			

Possum party

Any youngster will find hanging around is extra fun with this wallet or notepad cover with possum design.

The striking colour combination of yellow Aida fabric and sea-green bias binding means you'll never lose this cross-stitched wallet.

Size Cover 10 x 10 cm, width of spine 3 cm; motif about 5 x 4.5 cm

MATERIALS

30 cm square piece of pale yellow 14-count Aida fabric

DMC embroidery cottons in the colours indicated on the colour key

Tapestry needle size 24

1 m sea-green bias binding

8 cm square notepad (if desired)

METHOD

With running stitches, mark a 10 x 23 cm rectangle on the Aida fabric, and cut out with generous seam allowance. Also cut two 10 cm square Aida pieces for the pockets.

Fold the rectangular piece in half and crease the fold.

Open out the piece and, following the graph, embroider the motif in cross stitch in the centre of the front (the right-hand half). Work each cross over one fabric square, using two strands of embroidery cotton. When the embroidery is completed, cut around the embroidered piece on the marked outline.

TO ASSEMBLE

Finish one side of the small Aida pieces with bias binding. Place the two small pieces on either end of the embroidered piece, with wrong sides facing and raw edges aligned. Round the corners, and finish the edges with bias binding. If desired, insert the notepad.

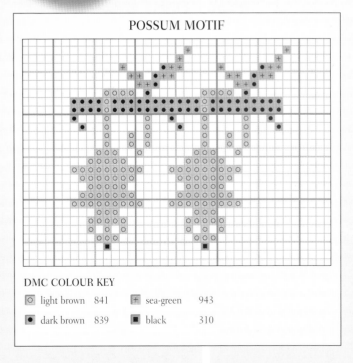

POSSUM MOTIF

DMC COLOUR KEY

⊙ light brown	841	✚ sea-green	943
● dark brown	839	▪ black	310

Olympic gold

Give baby a start in the race of life by adding one of these colourful motifs to a bought or specially made item. And for an extra touch the bottle warmer and bibs are made in the Olympic colours.

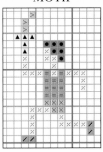

TORCH BEARER MOTIF

DMC COLOUR KEY

●	black	310
✕	red	606
╱	green	701
▲	yellow	725
⊠	pink	776
=	blue	798
▷	orange	947

BOTTLE COVER

Size About 25 cm high, base 9 cm diameter (If necessary, adapt the measurements of the cover for a different-sized bottle.)

MATERIALS

10 x 30 cm white hardanger fabric with nine double fabric threads per 1 cm

14.5 x 30 cm strip and 4 x 28 cm strip in yellow cotton fabric

5.5 x 30 cm strip and 11 cm diameter circle in blue cotton fabric

26 x 30 cm piece and 11 cm diameter circle in white towelling

40 cm red bias binding

60 cm green cord

DMC stranded embroidery cottons in the colours of the motif

Tapestry needle size 24

EMBROIDERY

Following the graph, embroider the torch bearer motif in cross stitch in the centre of the hardanger fabric. Position it 4 cm from the lower edge (one long side). Work each cross over two double fabric threads, using three strands of embroidery cotton. Leave a space of six double fabric threads below the motif, and work one row each of blue, yellow, red, green and black cross stitches over the entire width, allowing a space of two double fabric threads between each row.

TO ASSEMBLE

Work with right sides facing, and use 1 cm wide seams. Sew the wide yellow strip along the top edge, and the blue strip along the bottom edge of the embroidered hardanger strip. Baste the towelling to the back of this piece. Fold the ends of the remaining yellow strip 1 cm inwards, and stitch down. Fold under the long edges, and sew the strip onto the large yellow piece, positioning it 4 cm from the top edge and 2 cm from the sides; leave the ends of the strip open to form a casing.

Finish the top edge of the cover with red bias binding. Fold the cover double across its width, and sew the side seam. Finish the top section of the seam with red bias binding.

Baste the blue cotton and white towelling circles together, and sew the (double) circle inside the tube. Turn right side out. Thread the cord through the casing and knot the cord ends.

SINGLET

Size Motif about 3 x 3.5 cm

MATERIALS

White baby singlet

6 cm square piece of 10-count waste canvas (ten stitches to 2.5 cm)

DMC stranded embroidery cottons in black (310), red (606), pink (776), and blue (798)

Crewel needle size 8

EMBROIDERY

Baste canvas over right side of the singlet, over the area to be embroidered. Following the graph, embroider the weight-lifter motif in cross stitch, but omit the lower line. Work each cross through both layers over two fabric threads, using three strands of embroidery cotton.

This racy bottle cover is made in the five Olympic colours and decorated with a cross-stitched torch bearer.

Keep the needle perpendicular to the canvas while working, and stitch only through the canvas holes, not the canvas threads. Work the braces and weight bar in back stitch, using three

strands of cotton in the same colour as the pants.

When the embroidery is completed, dampen the canvas and then remove the basting and canvas threads one by one with tweezers.

WASHMITTEN

Size Motif about 3 x 4.5 cm

MATERIALS

White washmitten (or use washer if preferred)

About 7 cm square piece of 10-count waste canvas (ten stitches to 2.5 cm)

DMC stranded embroidery cottons in the colours of the motif

Crewel needle size 8

EMBROIDERY

Baste the canvas onto the washmitten over the area to be embroidered. Following the graph, embroider the swimmer motif in cross stitch. Work each cross through both layers over

two canvas threads, using three strands of embroidery cotton. Keep the needle perpendicular to the canvas while working, and stitch only through the canvas holes, not the canvas threads.

When completed, dampen the canvas and remove the basting and canvas threads one by one with tweezers.

BIB

Size About 18 x 22 cm

MATERIALS

20 x 25 cm piece of white hardanger fabric with nine double fabric threads per 1 cm

20 x 25 cm piece of white flannel or towelling

70 cm blue or green bias binding

65 cm yellow or red bias binding

DMC stranded embroidery cottons in the colours indicated on the colour key

Tapestry needle size 24

A swimmer is such a suitable motif for bath-room articles such as a washmitten.

SWIMMER MOTIF

WEIGHT-LIFTER MOTIF

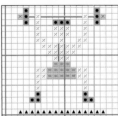

DMC COLOUR KEY

⦿	black	310
☒	red	606
▨	green	701
▲	yellow	725
⊠	pink	776
⊟	blue	798
▷	orange	947

OUTLINES

☐	blue	798
☐	red	606

Bouncing babies will love this embroidered weight-lifter.

CUTTING OUT

Enlarge the pattern graph for the bib and cut out the paper pattern. Cut one bib piece in white towelling. Outline the pattern with running stitches on the hardanger fabric.

EMBROIDERY

Following the desired graph, embroider the gymnasts motif or a row of weight-lifters in cross stitch, in the centre of the marked shape, about 5.5 cm from the lower marked line. Work each cross over two double fabric threads, using three strands of embroidery cotton. If using the weight-lifters motif, allow a space of four double fabric threads between each figure, and vary the colour of the pants. When the cross stitching is completed, use back stitch and three strands of cotton to add the details: for the weight-lifters, work the braces and bar of the weights in the colour of the pants; for the gymnasts, work the hair ribbons in the same colour as the suits and work all other outlines in yellow. When finished, cut the

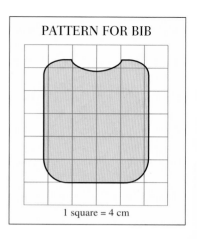

PATTERN FOR BIB

1 square = 4 cm

embroidered piece on the marked outline.

TO ASSEMBLE

Baste the bib and towelling lining together with wrong sides facing. Finish the outer edge with blue or green bias binding. Finish the neck edge with yellow or red bias binding; extend the binding at each side to form ties. Sew the folded edge of the binding together and knot the tie ends.

Gymnasts or weight-lifters make ideal motifs for these colourful bibs.

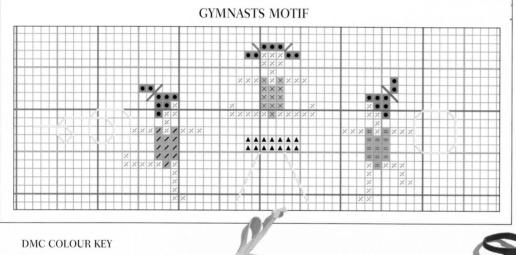

GYMNASTS MOTIF

DMC COLOUR KEY

●	black	310
✕	red	606
✓	green	701
▲	yellow	725
⊡	pink	776
☰	blue	798

OUTLINES

▢	red	606
▢	green	701
▢	yellow	725
▢	blue	798

Strawberry, apple and ice-cream — these motifs are truly delicious.

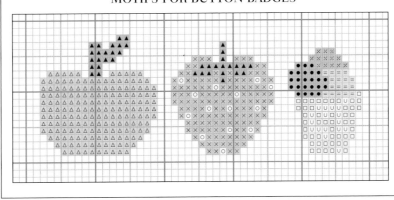

A button badge is very useful—it can be changed from outfit to outfit.

Size 6 cm diameter

MATERIALS

6 cm diameter button badge

10 cm square piece of white 11-count Aida fabric

Piece of felt or flannel same size as badge

DMC stranded embroidery cottons in the colours indicated on the colour key

Tapestry needle size 24

EMBROIDERY

Following the graph, embroider the desired motif in the centre of the fabric. Work in cross stitch over one fabric square, using three strands of embroidery cotton.

ASSEMBLY

Cover the front of the button with a same sized piece of felt or flannel. Cut the embroidered fabric piece 1 cm larger all around than the button, with the motif exactly in the centre. Stretch the embroidery around the button and secure it with large stitches at the back, but make sure that the pin can still be used freely.

MOTIFS FOR BUTTON BADGES

DMC COLOUR KEY

△	light green	703
▲	dark green	909
✕	red	666
○	yellow	307
⋃	light brown	725
▢	medium brown	783
⧄	dark brown	433
●	medium green	700
▤	pink	602

General instructions

FABRICS

All projects state the required type and amount of fabric. Counted cross stitch requires the use of a fabric with an even weave, so that the threads may be easily counted as you stitch from the graph. Usually one square on the graph is equal to one stitch. On linen this stitch is commonly worked over two threads, on Aida over one square, and on hardanger fabric over one pair of double threads. Check each project, however, for any specific instructions given.

Evenweave fabrics should have the required number of threads to the centimetre. To check this lay the fabric flat, then mark 1 cm (or 1 inch, whichever you prefer) with two pins. Count the number of threads between the two pins. This will give you the thread count, which is not necessarily the stitch count of your fabric. The inch equivalents of the metric names of linen (10-count linen has ten threads to the centimetre) are given here for your guidance.

8-count linen has 20 threads to the inch
10-count linen has 25 or 26 threads to the inch
11-count linen has 28 threads to the inch
12-count linen has 30 threads to the inch
13-count linen has 32 threads to the inch
14-count linen has 35 threads to the inch
16-count linen has 40 threads to the inch

Hardanger fabric is specially woven in double threads. Hardanger fabric has nine double threads to 1 cm or twenty-two double threads to the inch.

Aida fabric is specially woven into blocks, to give squares for stitching. Aida is very popular for working counted thread work and comes in a variety of colours. The different Aida fabrics are referred to by the number of squares to the inch: the larger the number the more squares per inch and so the finer the fabric. Aida is available in 11, 14, 16 and 18 count. Aida is also available in a band, sometimes referred to as *Ribband*. This 14-count band and 15-count band comes in three different widths, 3 cm, 5 cm and 8 cm and can be purchased in any length. The long edges of the band are already finished, often with a coloured edging.

If you have difficulty obtaining a particular fabric colour, dye a piece of white fabric with Dylon hot-water dye. Be sure to always follow the manufacturers directions and test a sample piece first.

WASTE CANVAS

Waste canvas is available in embroidery shops and allows you to work counted embroidery on any background fabric that does not have a natural grid for counting. Waste canvas is also available in different counts: 8, 10, 12 and 14 (stitches per inch). Purchase a piece of waste canvas larger than your design. Centre, then tack the canvas in place over the area where the design is to be stitched. Stitch the design, making sure you work through both layers of fabric. When the stitching is complete, totally dampen your work, then remove the waste canvas threads singly, horizontally and vertically, using a pair of tweezers. You will be left with the cross-stitch design on your chosen fabric.

THREADS

Many types of thread are available for embroidery. The embroidery thread most used is *stranded cotton,* which comes in a skein of approximately 8 metres in length. There are six strands of thread in the skein. Cut the length you require (usually no more than 30 cm, otherwise the thread loses its sheen and becomes fluffy), then strand off the desired number of threads. Even if you are going to use all six threads, you should separate them and put them back together for shinier, smoother work.

Perle thread, also 100 per cent cotton, is a shiny twisted single thread that is used in hardanger embroidery. It comes in a variety of thicknesses: Perle 3, 5, 8 and 12. Perle 5, 8 and 12 are available in balls as well as skeins. The higher the number, the finer the thread.

NEEDLES AND PINS

For counted work on evenweave fabrics, tapestry needles (those with a blunt end) are used. They come in a variety of sizes, 18, 20, 22, 24 and 26, the larger the number the finer the needle. Never leave the needle in your fabric as it will eventually rust and leave a mark that is almost impossible to remove. This rule applies also to pins. Lace pins are suitable for work on good-quality fabrics as they are a very fine pin.

BEFORE YOU BEGIN

To prevent fraying, finish the edges of your fabric with machine zigzag or overlocking. Then find the centre of your fabric by folding it in half horizontally and vertically and tack along these lines. Find the centre of the design—usually it is marked at the top and bottom of the graph. Where the centre is unmarked, count the squares of the total design's height and width and divide by two. Start wherever you like, but many find that the centre is simplest, working outwards in each direction following the chart square by square.

Beginners are advised to use an embroidery hoop to keep the fabric taut, and many experienced cross stitchers continue this practice. To prevent damage to fabric, bind the inner ring of the hoop with cotton tape. Take your work out of the hoop when you have finished a cross stitching session or the fabric will become distorted. To avoid rust marks, remember to remove your needle whenever you put your project aside.

Cut threads no longer than 30 cm; longer threads tend to lose their sheen and fray. Threads should be separated and then allowed to retwist. While stitching, occasionally stop and drop the needle to let the threads relax. Never use knots as they will show

through and leave ugly irregularities. Secure your thread on the wrong side with the first few stitches. When you are finishing off, weave your thread through a few stitches in the back of the work.

WORKING CROSS STITCH

Bring the needle up from the back of the fabric at the lower left corner of the centre square. Leave thread (twice the length of the needle) on the back of the work and hold it so that it will be overcast as you work the first few stitches; snip off excess. Continue by pushing the needle down through the upper right corner of the square. Repeat the procedure until you come to the end of the row on the graph. Then bring the needle up through the lower right corner and down through the upper left corner of this last square and cover all the diagonal stitches to make crosses.

When the first row of cross stitches is complete, continue with your selected thread and bring the needle up through the lower left-hand hole of the first square to be stitched in the row below. Work as before, making sure always to work crosses in the same direction for an even finish. Finish off the colour by

running the needle under about four stitches at the back of the work, then cut the thread.

Do not carry the thread across long distances at the back, especially when these areas are not covered with stitches, as the threads will show through unattractively on the front of the work.

WORKING BACK STITCH

When stitched on Aida cloth, back stitch is regulated by the even weave and it is easy to keep the resulting stitches the same length. It is most often used in conjunction with cross stitch to make a straight outline or give emphasis to the cross stitch motif. Usually it is worked with one strand of thread whereas cross stitch is worked with two strands.

WASHING YOUR EMBROIDERY

Always work with clean hands. If the project becomes soiled, gently hand wash it using pure soap, rinse it thoroughly in cold water, blot it with a towel and leave it to dry in the shade. Before pressing it, place a towel on the ironing board to pad it. Lay the embroidery face down on it, cover with a thin cloth and press lightly.

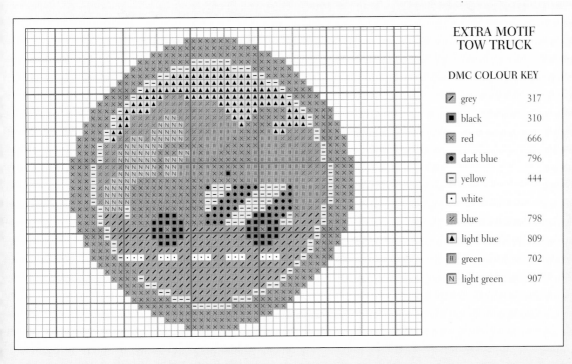

EXTRA MOTIF TOW TRUCK

DMC COLOUR KEY

✏	grey	317
■	black	310
✗	red	666
●	dark blue	796
⊟	yellow	444
⊡	white	
✖	blue	798
▲	light blue	809
‖	green	702
N	light green	907

Stitch library

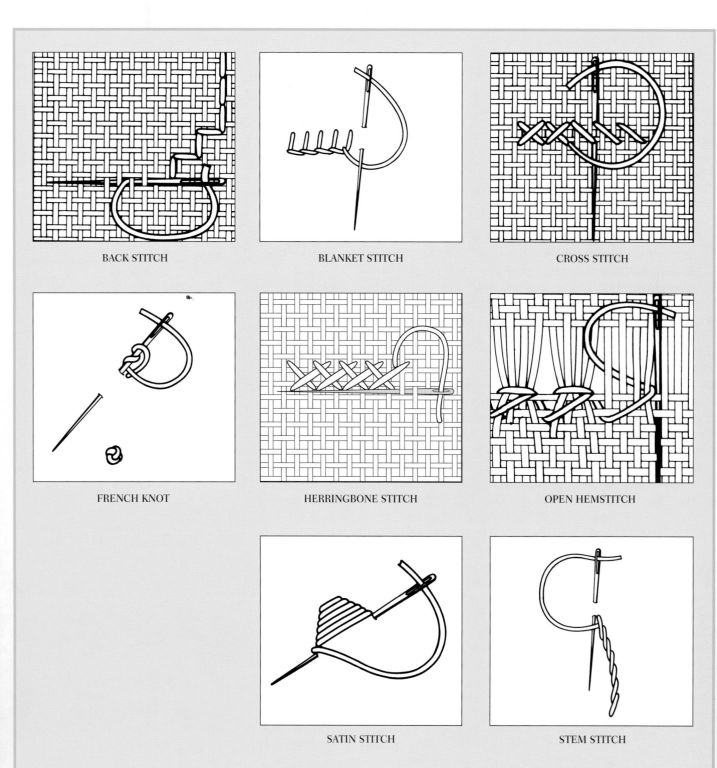

BACK STITCH

BLANKET STITCH

CROSS STITCH

FRENCH KNOT

HERRINGBONE STITCH

OPEN HEMSTITCH

SATIN STITCH

STEM STITCH

Index

Published by Murdoch Books®, a division of Murdoch Magazines Pty Ltd,
213 Miller Street, North Sydney NSW 2060

Designer: Di Quick
Project Managing Editor: Christine Eslick
Translation and new projects: Marianne Porteners
Motif designs: Marianne Porteners (pages 35, 37, 48, 59, 62, 82); Lorraine Hannay (pages 31, 39, 56 (emus), 75, 103); all others Ariadne/Holland
Photography (new projects): Sue Stubbs
Graphs: Alison Snepp
Diagrams: Lorenzo Lucia

Publisher: Anne Wilson
Publishing Manager: Catie Ziller
Managing Editor: Susan Tomnay
Craft Editor: Alison Snepp
Art Director: Lena Lowe
Production Co-ordinator: Liz Fitzgerald
International Manager: Mark Newman
Marketing Manager: Mark Smith
National Sales Manager: Keith Watson
Key Accounts Sales Manager: Kim Deacon
Photo Librarian: Dianne Bedford

National Library of Australia
Cataloguing-in-Publication Data
Quick cross stitch
Includes index
ISBN 0 86411 413 3
1. Cross-stitch—Patterns
746.443021

Printed by Prestige Litho, Queensland

First published 1995

Australian distribution to supermarkets and newsagents by Gordon & Gotch Ltd,
68 Kingsgrove Road, Belmore NSW 2192

Every effort has been made to ensure the availability of materials in this book, but the availability of particular thread colours and fabrics cannot be guaranteed.

Cover: A selection of projects from the book.
Inside front cover: Red and blue teapots on Aida potholders (pages 62–3).
Title page: Handkerchiefs with initial or rosebud (pages 50–1).